Introduction

This book offers a cooperative, engaging approach to meet and exceed the middle school and high school Language Arts Standards set forth by the National Council for Teachers of English and the International Reading Association. The standards establish expectations for students and teachers. However, teachers have wide latitude for how they teach to reach academic goals. Many English/language arts teachers rely on traditional instructional strategies. The teacher lectures or leads the class in discussions. While a direct instruction model has a place in every language classroom, it is not the only mode of instruction, nor always the best.

Language arts standards call for comprehension, interpretation, and evaluation of texts. The standards encourage speaking skills and effective communication. And they ask that students participate as knowledgeable, reflective, creative, and critical members of a variety of literacy communities. Cooperative instructional strategies provide students the opportunities to interact, discuss, tutor, and practice their communication skills in a way not possible without student-to-student interaction. Breaking the class into smaller groups and into pairs gives each student more opportunities to participate. Instead of being in one large class, the student is now one in a small group or even one in a pair. In the teacher-led classroom, there is only one or two active participants in the class at a time—the teacher and a student. In the cooperative learning classroom, there is at least one student in every pair or team that is actively engaged. When we look at how much more engaged students are in cooperative groups, it is no wonder they learn more, keep on task more, and enjoy learning more.

In addition to the quantity of interactions, look too at the quality of interactions in the cooperative classroom. Student-to-student interactions can be used to deepen students' understanding of texts and language arts content. Explaining a concept or discussing a book makes the content more meaningful and memorable. Interactions empower students to become active learners, rather than passive recipients of information. To learn something well, students must be engaged and active, asking questions and discussing their learning. Students learn best by doing. The activities in this book are based on Kagan Cooperative

Cooperative Learning Structures boost active engagement. More active learning enhances motivation and promotes language arts content mastery and skill development.

Learning Structures—si... promote student interact... curriculum. The structur... cooperation, quizzing, pe... effective processes for mastering the language arts content. The structures are designed to engage every student in learning. Each student plays an active role with each structure, thereby increasing the probability of success for even reluctant learners. Students who might not fully participate in a whole-class setting are now highly encouraged to participate on an ongoing basis. The structure of the task requires everyone to keep tuned in and stay on task.

Most students enjoy the opportunities to interact with peers and find cooperative learning more motivating. Some structures are whole-class interactions; others are completed in small groups or in pairs. These structures provide review, self-assessment, class discussion, and skill development.

Book Organization

Eight Kagan Cooperative Learning Structures are presented throughout this book. Step-by-step instructions and tips are provided to make it easy to learn and use each structure in your classroom. The structures were selected because they are particularly good for teaching and learning language arts content. For example, Think-Write-RoundRobin is a fun and engaging way for students to review need-to-know language arts curriculum. Timed Pair Share provides the opportunity for students to practice communication skills and share information and knowledge.

Following each structure are a number of activities and resource pages to use with the structure. The content provided is a sampling of language arts curriculum and skills for grades 7–12. The ready-to-use activities allow you to try the various structures. We hope you will try the sample activities provided and witness firsthand the powerful impact the structures have on student motivation and learning. There are also a number of blackline templates for you to create your own materials to use with the structures. It is our hope that not only will you use the ready-to-use activities provided, but also learn the structures well and integrate these active learning strategies frequently into your daily teaching.

Acknowledgments

The materials for this book are a compilation of Structure lessons based on Language Arts Standards for grades 7–12. A project such as this cannot be completed without the assistance of others.

This book has grown through years of teaching experiences and ideas shared through conversations with colleagues and teammates. Other ideas have been developed through attendance at educational workshops and conferences.

A thank-you to my friend and former colleague, Alisa Krehbiel, for testing some of the activities and providing valuable feedback.

This book would not have come to fruition without the encouragement and guidance of Dr. Jacqueline Minor, Director of School Improvement Programs for Kagan Professional Development. Her assistance, insights, and constructive feedback have given me confidence in completing this work.

Appreciation goes to Miguel Kagan, Director of Publications, for believing in me and editing the manuscript. Thanks to his team of designers: Alex Core, Book Designer; Heather Malk, Contributing Designer; Becky Herrington, Publications Manager; Erin Kant, Illustrator; and Kim Fields, Copy Editor.

Table of Contents

Structure 1
Carousel Review........... 11

Structure 2
Find Someone Who.......27

Structure 3
Mix-N-Match 41

Structure 4
Showdown 99

Structure 5
Simultaneous RoundTable 137

Structure 6
Team Word-Webbing............................ 165

Structure 7
Think-Write-RoundRobin 181

Structure 8
Timed Pair Share 197

Chart of
Language Arts Elements

	Pages	Characters	Text Types	Novel Elements	Vocabulary
Carousel Review					
The Diary of Anne Frank—Compare and Contrast Characterization Charts	14–16	★	★	★	★
The Adventures of Tom Sawyer—Novel Quotes Review	17–18	★		★	
The Giver—Novel Review	19	★		★	
Elements of a Novel	20			★	
Character Analysis	21	★		★	
The House on Mango Street—Novel Quotes Review	22			★	
Snow Falling on Cedars—Problems and Dilemmas Characters Face	23	★			★
Novel Review—Five W's and How Questions	24			·	
Find Someone Who					
Getting Acquainted	30	★			·
Literature Hunt	31	★		·	
The Adventures of Tom Sawyer—Novel Discussion Prompts	32	·			
Figurative Language Identification	33–34				·
Novel Review—Generating Questions	35	·		·	
Parts of Speech	36				·
Elements of a Novel or Story	37	★		·	
Vocabulary Builder	38				·
"To Build a Fire"—Short Story Review	39	·		·	
Mix-N-Match					
Reading Terms	44–49	★		★	★
Root Words	50–54				★
Root Words and Meanings	55–60				★
Similes	61–67				★
Prefixes and Suffixes	68–72				★

Chart of
Language Arts Elements *(continued)*

	Pages	Characters	Text Types	Novel Elements	Vocabulary
Mix-N-Match (continued)					
Prefixes	73–77				★
Synonyms	78–82				★
Figurative Language	83–87				★
Parts of Speech	88–96				★
Showdown					
The Prefix Is…	102–108				★
Prefix Examples	109–114				★
Text Structure Signal Words	115–124		★		
Text Structures and Types	125–133		★		
Simultaneous RoundTable					
Punctuation	140–145				★
Antonyms and Synonyms	146–151				★
Vocabulary Builder	152				★
Types of Irony	153–154			★	
Literary Devices	155			★	
Novel Study	156–157				
Thinking Questions	158			★	
Literature Graphic Organizers	159–163	★	★	★	
Team Word-Webbing					
Vocabulary Word-Web	168	★		★	★
Character Word-Web	169	★		★	★
Figurative Language Word-Web	170		★	★	★
Story Elements Word-Web	171			★	
Parts of Speech Word-Web	172				★
Punctuation Word-Web	173				★
Literary Periods Word-Web	174			★	
Poetry Word-Web	175		★	★	
Julius Caesar—Word-Web	176	★		★	
The Grapes of Wrath—Word-Web	177	★		★	
Catch 22—Character Word-Web	178	★			
William Shakespeare Word-Web	179	★		★	

Chart of
Language Arts Elements (continued)

	Pages	Characters	Text Types	Novel Elements	Vocabulary
Think-Write-RoundRobin					
The Great Gatsby—Analyzing Quotes	184	★		★	
The Catcher in the Rye—Analyzing Quotes	185	★		★	
The Pearl—Predicting Meaning Before Reading	186–187	★		★	
The Great Gatsby—Symbolism	188	★		★	
Prefixes	189				★
Suffixes	190				★
Word Definitions 1 and 2	191–192				★
Character Chart—*A Lesson Before Dying*	193	★		★	
Reading Strategy: Before and After	194–195	★		★	★
Timed Pair Share					
Novel Review Questions—Any Novel	200–201	★		★	
Poetry Analysis Questions	202–203	★	★	★	★
The Giver—Novel Review Questions	204–205	★		★	
Of Mice and Men—Discussion Prompts	206–207	★		★	

English Standards for Language Arts

National Council for Teachers of English
International Reading Association

1. Students read a wide range of print and non-print texts to build an understanding of texts, of themselves, and of the cultures of the United States and the world; to acquire new information; to respond to the needs and demands of society and the workplace; and for personal fulfillment. Among these texts are fiction and nonfiction, and classic and contemporary works.

2. Students read a wide range of literature from many periods in many genres to build an understanding of the many dimensions (e.g., philosophical, ethical, aesthetic) of human experience.

3. Students apply a wide range of strategies to comprehend, interpret, evaluate, and appreciate texts. They draw on their prior experience, their interactions with other readers and writers, their knowledge of word meaning and of other texts, their word identification strategies, and their understanding of textual features (e.g., sound-letter correspondence, sentence structure, context, graphics).

4. Students adjust their use of spoken, written, and visual language (e.g., conventions, style, vocabulary) to communicate effectively with a variety of audiences and for different purposes.

5. Students employ a wide range of strategies as they write and use different writing process elements appropriately to communicate with different audiences for a variety of purposes.

6. Students apply knowledge of language structure, language conventions (e.g., spelling, punctuation), media techniques, figurative language, and genre to create, critique, and discuss print and non-print texts.

7. Students conduct research on issues and interests by generating ideas and questions, and by posing problems. They gather, evaluate, and synthesize data from a variety of sources (e.g., print and non-print texts, artifacts, people) to communicate their discoveries in ways that suit their purpose and audience.

8. Students use a variety of technological and informational resources (e.g., libraries, databases, computer networks, video) to gather and synthesize information and to create and communicate knowledge.

9. Students develop an understanding of and respect for diversity in language use, patterns, and dialects across cultures, ethnic groups, geographic regions, and social roles.

10. Students whose first language is not English make use of their first language to develop competency in the English language arts and to develop understanding of content across the curriculum.

11. Students participate as knowledgeable, reflective, creative, and critical members of a variety of literacy communities.

12. Students use spoken, written, and visual language to accomplish their own purposes (e.g., learning, enjoyment, persuasion, the exchange of information).

Carousel Review

Structure I

Structure 1
Carousel Review

Teams rotate to discuss and record information on various topics.

Group Size
Teams of Four

 **Steps**

Setup: One marker per team, each a different color. Teacher posts one chart per team around the room. Each chart is labeled with a different review topic.

1 **Teams Discuss First Review Topic**
Each team stands in front of a different chart, discussing what they know about the topic. No writing.

2 **Recorders Record Team Disussion**
One teammate records team's thoughts for 1 minute.

3 **Teams Rotate**
Teacher calls stop and teams rotate to the next topic chart.

4 **Teams Review and Discuss**
For a pre-set time period, teams read remarks left by prior team, and discuss what they would like to add. No writing.

5 **New Recorders Record**
A new Recorder records thoughts or queries of the team for 1 minute.

6 **Continue Rotating**
Rotations continue until teams review all topics.

7 **Display Review Charts**
Review charts remain available for study.

Tips
- Give each team a different colored marker to identify each team's contribution.
- Space the review charts far enough apart to give teams space to discuss topics without interference.
- Randomly select a Recorder, then rotate Recorder role using student numbers.
- Give students a worksheet with the review topics to fill out before they do Carousel Review.
- Create one chart for each team.

Activities

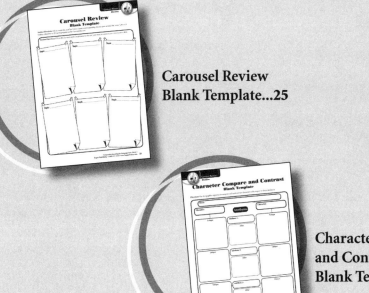

Carousel Review
Blank Template...25

Character Compare
and Contrast
Blank Template...26

The Diary of Anne Frank
Compare and Contrast Characterization Charts

TEACHER INSTRUCTIONS

Teams use Carousel Review to discuss and respond to comments pertaining to the novel, **The Diary of Anne Frank.**

1 Prepare six charts on the personality, behaviors, and relationships of Mr. Frank and Mr. van Daan. (See page 15.) Post charts around the room.

2 Give each student a handout (page 15) and some time to fill out their own information about Mr. Frank and Mr. van Daan.

3 Teams are given a different colored marker. Each team stands in front of one of the charts posted around the room.

4 Teams discuss the character. Randomly select one team member to be the Recorder. The Recorder records the team's ideas.

5 At teacher's signal (maybe 1–2 minutes per chart), groups rotate one chart to the right.

6 The marker is given to a different team member who is now the Recorder.

7 Team reads the heading for the new chart. As teams encounter charts with information, they will first review other teams' comments. They add a question mark (?) if they question the response or idea. They add a plus (+) sign if they agree with the comments. Next, they discuss additional ideas.

8 Team has 1–2 minutes to record information for this character.

9 When time is up, have teams rotate to a new chart, review comments of prior teams, then discuss and record new ideas.

10 Continue rotating until teams have recorded on each chart. When groups have rotated to each chart, tell teams to return to their seats.

Extension Ideas

At this point the teacher may choose to have individuals complete the Characterization Chart organizer comparing the two characters. Or the teacher may:

- Hold a class discussion and have students complete the organizer during the discussion.
- Have teams take their organizer and again rotate from chart to chart at teacher's signal to determine information they want to add to their organizer.
- Suggest that students review the text to add information and support their points.

As an independent task, students will write a Compare and Contrast essay about Mr. Frank and Mr. van Daan using the organizer information. The teacher will determine the essay writing style.

The Diary of Anne Frank
Characterization Charts

Teacher Directions: Create charts based on the attributes of Mr. Frank and Mr. Van Daan. Post the charts around the room. Copy a handout for each student to fill in information about the characters before they rotate to the charts as a team.

Student Directions: Fill in ideas about the characters. Be prepared to discuss your ideas in teams as you rotate to each chart.

Mr. Frank's Personality

Mr. van Daan's Personality

Mr. Frank's Behaviors

Mr. van Daan's Behaviors

Mr. Frank's Relationship to Others in Annex

Mr. van Daan's Relationship to Others in Annex

The Diary of Anne Frank
Characterization Compare and Contrast Chart

Directions: Use this graphic organizer to compare and contrast Mr. Frank and Mr. van Daan, with respect to their personalities, behaviors, and relationships.

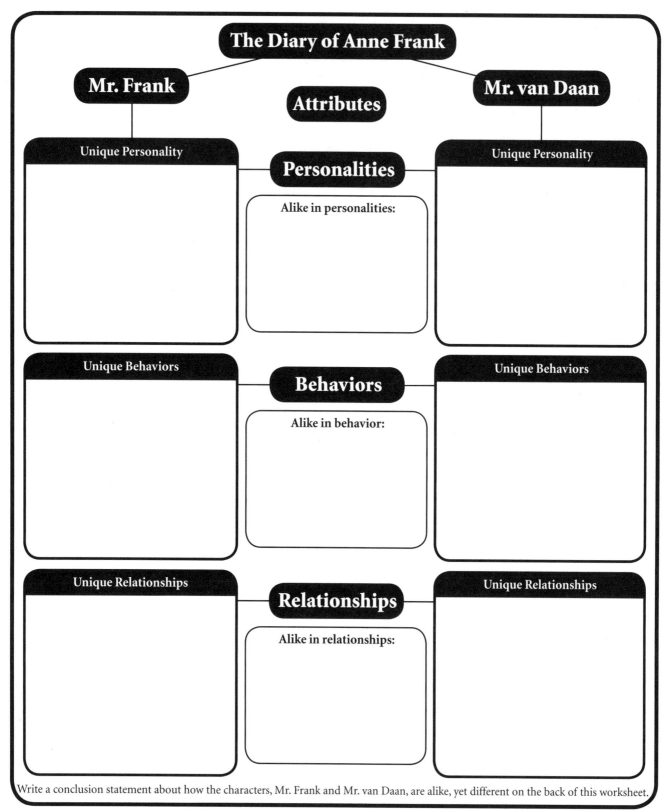

The Diary of Anne Frank

Mr. Frank

Attributes

Mr. van Daan

Unique Personality	Personalities	Unique Personality
	Alike in personalities:	

Unique Behaviors	Behaviors	Unique Behaviors
	Alike in behavior:	

Unique Relationships	Relationships	Unique Relationships
	Alike in relationships:	

Write a conclusion statement about how the characters, Mr. Frank and Mr. van Daan, are alike, yet different on the back of this worksheet.

The Adventures of Tom Sawyer
Novel Quotes Review

TEACHER INSTRUCTIONS

Teams use Carousel Review to discuss and respond to quotes in the novel, **The Adventures of Tom Sawyer.**

1 Write quotes from the novel at top of sheets of chart paper. There should be one quote per sheet of chart paper. (See page 18 for quotes.) Post the charts around the room.

2 Teams are given a different colored marker. Each team stands in front of a chart.

3 Teams discuss what they think the quote means, based on the text they have read.

4 Randomly select one team member to be the Recorder. The Recorder records the team's ideas.

5 At teacher's signal (maybe 1–2 minutes per chart), groups rotate one chart to the right.

6 The marker is given to a different team member who is now the Recorder.

7 Team reads the quote on the new chart. As teams encounter charts with information, they will first review other teams' comments. They add a question mark (?) if they question the response or idea. They add a plus (+) sign if they agree with the comments. Next, they discuss additional ideas.

8 Team has 1–2 minutes to record information about the quote.

9 When time is up, have teams rotate to a new chart, review comments of prior teams, then discuss and record new ideas.

10 Continue rotating until teams have recorded on each chart. When groups have rotated to each chart, tell teams to return to their seats.

Questions to consider for responding to quotes:

1. Who is talking?

2. What leads up to the statement or situation?

3. What is going on at the time the quote or situation is happening?

The Adventures of Tom Sawyer
Novel Quotes Review

Teacher Directions: Create charts with one quote on each from the novel, *The Adventures of Tom Sawyer*. Copy a handout for each student to fill in ideas about the quotes.

Student Directions: Fill in ideas about each quotation. Be prepared to discuss your ideas in teams as you rotate to each chart.

"Go away and leave me alone, can't you! I hate you!"

"Be so mean if you want to! I know something that's going to happen…."

"Little hands, and weak—but they've helped Muff Potter a power, and they'd help him more if they could."

"Tom was out late that night and came to bed through the window."

"Tom was a glittering hero once more—the pet of the old, the envy of the young. His name even went into immortal print, for the village paper magnified him. There were some that believed he would be president, yet, if he escaped hanging."

"Huck Finn's wealth and the fact that he was now under the Widow Douglas's protection introduced him into society—no, dragged him into it, hurled him into it—and his sufferings were almost more than he could bear."

The Giver
Novel Review

Teacher Directions: After reading the novel, *The Giver*, by Lois Lowry, create a chart for each topic as a review of the novel. Post charts around the room. Copy a handout for each student to fill in ideas about the novel.

Student Directions: Fill in ideas about *The Giver*. Be prepared to discuss your ideas in teams as you rotate to each chart.

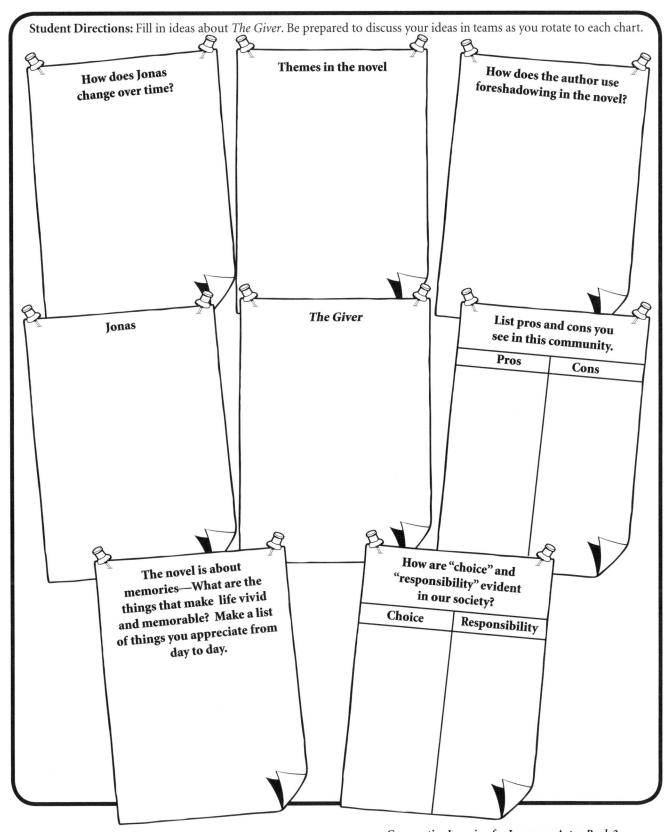

How does Jonas change over time?

Themes in the novel

How does the author use foreshadowing in the novel?

Jonas

The Giver

List pros and cons you see in this community.

Pros	Cons

The novel is about memories—What are the things that make life vivid and memorable? Make a list of things you appreciate from day to day.

How are "choice" and "responsibility" evident in our society?

Choice	Responsibility

Elements of a Novel

Teacher Directions: Create a chart for each novel element. Post the charts around the room. Copy a handout for each student to fill in information from a novel they have read.

Student Directions: Fill in ideas from the novel you have read. Be prepared to discuss your ideas in teams as you rotate to each chart.

Novel _____

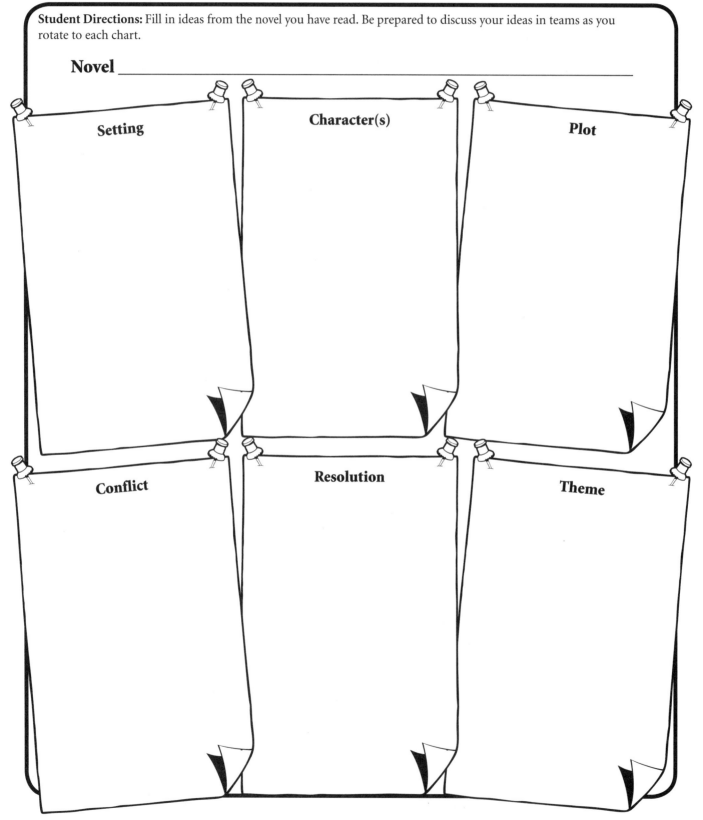

Setting

Character(s)

Plot

Conflict

Resolution

Theme

Character Analysis

Teacher Directions: Create a chart on different dimensions of a character from a novel students have read. Post the charts around the room. Teams may be assigned unique characters.

Student Directions: Fill in information about your assigned character. Be prepared to discuss your ideas in teams as you rotate to each chart.

Novel _____ Character_____

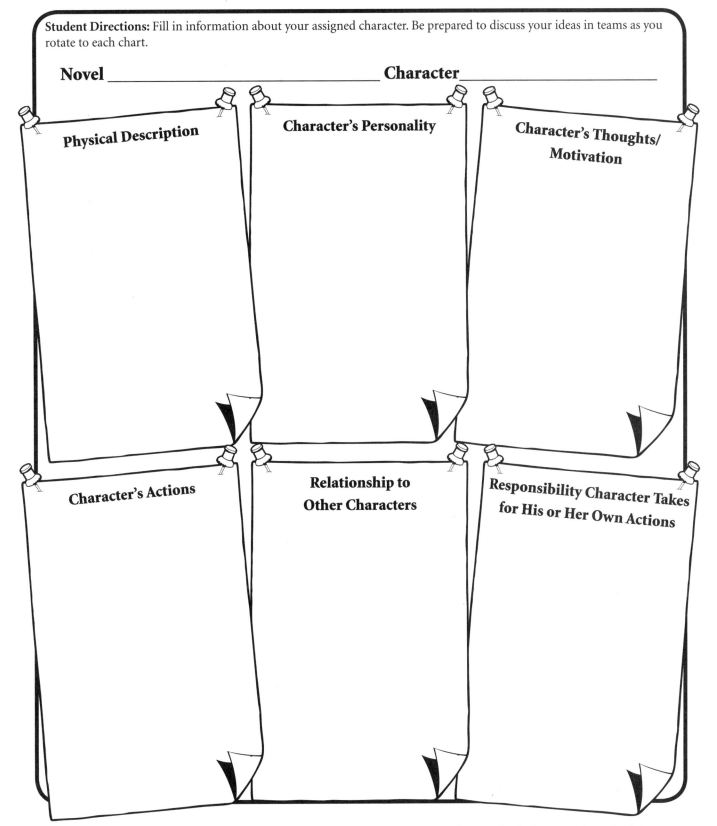

Physical Description

Character's Personality

Character's Thoughts/ Motivation

Character's Actions

Relationship to Other Characters

Responsibility Character Takes for His or Her Own Actions

The House on Mango Street
Novel Quotes Review

Teacher Directions: Create charts with quotes from the novel, *The House on Mango Street,* by Sandra Cisneros. Post the charts around the room. Copy a handout for each student to analyze quotes.

Student Directions: Analyze each quote. Be prepared to discuss your ideas in teams as you rotate to each chart.

"When you leave you must remember to come back for others."

"You must keep writing. It will keep you free...."

"I put it down on paper and then the ghost does not ache so much."

"Like it or not you are Mango Street, and one day you'll come back too."

"People who live on hills sleep so close to the stars they forget those of us who live too much on earth."

"Until then I am a red balloon, a balloon tied to an anchor."

Snow Falling on Cedars
Problems and Dilemmas Characters Face

Teacher Directions: Create a chart for each character in the novel, *Snow Falling on Cedars*, by David Guterson. Post the charts around the room. Copy a handout for each student to fill in problems and dilemmas characters faced.

Student Directions: Fill in problems and dilemmas each character faced. Be prepared to discuss your ideas in teams as you rotate to each chart.

Ishmael Chambers

Hatsue Miyamoto

Kabuo Miyamoto

Carl Heine, Jr.

Nels Gudmundsson

Alvin Hooks

Novel Review
The Five W's and How Questions

Teacher Directions: Create a chart for each question. Post the charts around the room. Copy a handout for each student to fill in ideas about the novel.

Student Directions: Fill in ideas about the novel associated with each question. Be prepared to discuss your ideas in teams as you rotate to each chart.

Novel _____

Who?

What?

When?

Where?

Why?

How?

Carousel Review
Blank Template

Teacher Directions: Fill in a topic for each box below. Create a corresponding chart to post around the room. Give each student a handout to fill out in preparation for Carousel Review.

Student Directions: Fill in ideas for each topic. Be prepared to discuss your ideas in teams as you rotate to each chart.

Topic _____

Topic _____

Topic _____

Topic _____

Topic _____

Topic _____

Character Compare and Contrast
Blank Template

Directions: Use this graphic organizer to compare and contrast two characters with respect to three attributes.

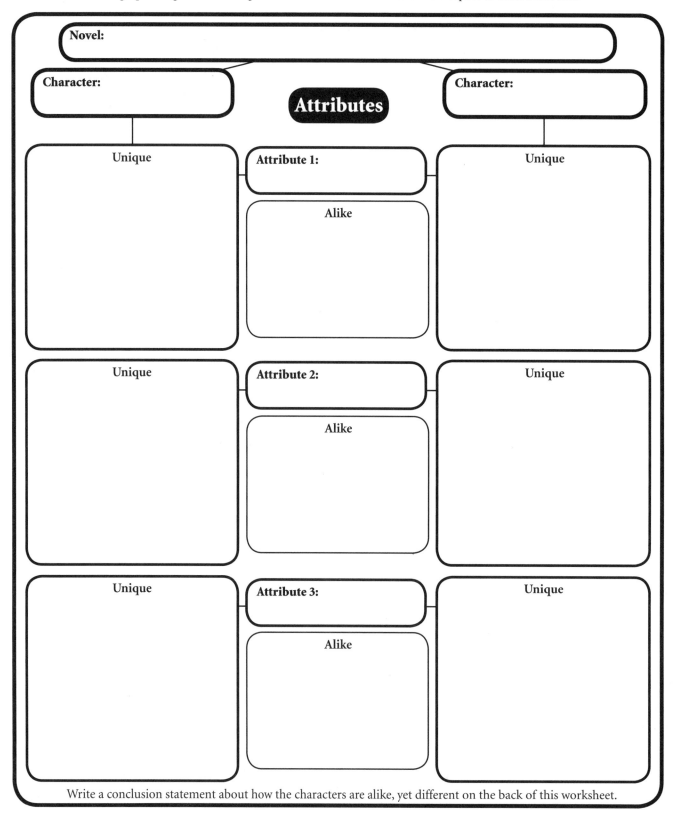

Novel:

Character:

Attributes

Character:

Unique

Attribute 1:

Alike

Unique

Unique

Attribute 2:

Alike

Unique

Unique

Attribute 3:

Alike

Unique

Write a conclusion statement about how the characters are alike, yet different on the back of this worksheet.

Find Someone Who

Structure 2

Find Someone Who

Students circulate through the classroom, forming and reforming pairs, trying to "find someone who" knows an answer, then they become "someone who knows."

Group Size
Whole Class

Steps

Setup: The teacher prepares a worksheet or questions for students.

1 Students Mix
Students mix in the class, keeping a hand raised until they find a partner that is not a teammate.

2 Partner A Asks Question
In pairs, Partner A asks a question from the worksheet; Partner B responds. Partner A records the answer on his or her own worksheet and expresses appreciation.

3 Partner B Checks
Partner B checks and initials the answer.

4 Partner B Asks Question
Partner B asks a question; Partner A responds. Partner B records the answer on his or her own worksheet and expresses appreciation.

5 Partner A Checks
Partner A checks and initials the answer.

6 Partners Depart
Partners shake hands, part, and raise a hand as they search for a new partner.

7 Continue Finding Someone Who
Students repeat Steps 1–6 until their worksheets are complete.

8 Students Are Seated
When their worksheets are complete, students sit down; seated students may be approached by others as a resource.

9 Teams Compare Answers
In teams, students compare answers; if there is disagreement or uncertainty, they raise four hands to ask a team question.

Tips
• Give students a task to complete if they finish before others.
• For students who may not know any answers to the worksheet, provide extra support in advance or give him or her one answer so he or she can be a resource for others.
• Pair up ESL students with a language twin, a partner who speaks English and the student's native language.
• Send students who need extra help out with a buddy.

Activities

**Find Someone Who
Blank Worksheet Template...40**

• I Ask
• You Answer
• I Write
• You Initial

Getting Acquainted

Directions: Students find a partner and ask a question from the worksheet. Partners respond and partners initial on the blank line.

Getting Acquainted Worksheet

Coolest vacation destination	Favorite fast food	Wears jewelry	New to this school	Describe family
___	___	___	___	___
Wears contacts or glasses	Favorite dessert	Describe how got name	Nickname or like to be called	Describe outfit today
___	___	___	___	___
Favorite color	Has a unique pet	Favorite activity	Favorite author	Favorite singing group
___	___	___	___	___
Favorite season	Dream car	Favorite actor	Best TV comedy	Best book I've read
___	___	___	___	___

• I Ask
• You Answer
• I Write
• You Initial

Find Someone Who
Blackline

Literature Hunt

Directions: Copy a handout for each student. Students pair up and ask each other one question from the handout. Students write answers on handout and initial on blank line.

Literature Hunt Worksheet

Two novels written by Charles Dickens: ① ② _____	Name two writers from the Romantic period: ① ② _____	Who wrote *Of Mice and Men*? Who is the main character of this novel? _____
Describe the main character in *The Call of the Wild*. _____	List two novels by the same author. Author: _____ ① Novel: _____ _____ ② Novel: _____ _____ _____	Name the main character in *To Kill a Mockingbird*. Name the author. _____
Ray Bradbury wrote… _____	Name and describe two symbols found in *The Great Gatsby*. ① ② _____	J. R. R. Tolkien wrote… _____
In *Night*, Ellie Wiesel writes about: ① What members of society? ② What time period in history? _____	In writing *The Grapes of Wrath*, Steinbeck addressed what social/economic issue? _____	List two plays by Arthur Miller: ① ② _____
List two novels by Mark Twain: ① ② _____	Who wrote *1984*? _____	What is a theme in Steinbeck's *The Pearl*? _____

The Adventures of Tom Sawyer
Novel Discussion Prompts

Directions: Copy a handout for each student. Students find a partner and ask each other one prompt from Twain's novel, *The Adventures of Tom Sawyer*. For each prompt, the responding student states: 1) how the prompt relates to the novel, and 2) how the prompt relates to his or her personal life. Partners then initial on blank line.

The Adventures of Tom Sawyer Worksheet

Has lived in Missouri	Has ever tried to run away	Has been in trouble with a friend	Has mother with only one sister	Has broken mother's precious dishes or possession
___	___	___	___	___
Has trouble memorizing information	Has had to decide about telling the truth about what they saw	Has a younger cousin who isn't always nice to you	Has built a raft	Has been away from home and scared
___	___	___	___	___
Has been lost	Has been rewarded for doing a good deed	Has camped out overnight	Has a best friend	Has had an adventurous vacation
___	___	___	___	___
Has traveled along the Mississippi River	Has been in a haunted house	Has been on an island	Has been to a live circus performance	Has enjoyed their childhood
___	___	___	___	___

• I Ask
• You Answer
• I Write
• You Initial

Find Someone Who
Blackline

Figurative Language
Identification

Directions: Copy a handout for each student. Students find a partner and ask the partner to identify the figurative language for one square. Partners respond then initial on the small blank line.

Figurative Language Worksheet

Simile • Personification • Alliteration • Hyperbole • Metaphor • Idiom • Onomatopoeia

She was happy as a clam.	I'm so tired you could knock me over with a feather.	When there's work to be done, Dan is an eager beaver.	The owl hooted as he flew from tree to tree.
The clouds wept as we said farewell to our dog Jake.	Laughing llamas lounge with loud leprechauns.	Sam beat me to a pulp in the ring.	The evening stars winked at us from the crystal clear sky.
I've told you a million times not to exaggerate.	The bear's steps were thunder as he marched through the woods.	Peter Piper picked a peck of pickled peppers.	My plans are to ace the test.
He was as mad as a hornet.	The bull was boiling mad.	The mosquito buzzed around my head as I hiked the path.	Round the ragged rock the rascal ran.
I'm at the end of my rope with planning for the trip.	I'm so hungry I could eat a horse.	The snake hissed as it slithered quickly through the grass.	The turn appeared as quick as a wink.

Figurative Language
Answer Key

Simile • Personification • Alliteration • Hyperbole • Metaphor • Idiom • Onomatopoeia

Figurative Language Answer Key

She was happy as a clam. **Simile**	I'm so tired you could knock me over with a feather. **Hyperbole**	When there's work to be done, Dan is an eager beaver. **Idiom**	The owl hooted as he flew from tree to tree. **Onomatopoeia**
The clouds wept as we said farewell to our dog Jake. **Personification**	Laughing llamas lounge with loud leprechauns. **Alliteration**	Sam beat me to a pulp in the ring. **Metaphor**	The evening stars winked at us from the crystal clear sky. **Personification**
I've told you a million times not to exaggerate. **Hyperbole**	The bear's steps were thunder as he marched through the woods. **Metaphor**	Peter Piper picked a peck of pickled peppers. **Alliteration**	My plans are to ace the test. **Idiom**
He was as mad as a hornet. **Simile**	The bull was boiling mad. **Metaphor**	The mosquito buzzed around my head as I hiked the path. **Onomatopoeia**	Round the ragged rock the rascal ran. **Alliteration**
I'm at the end of my rope with planning for the trip. **Idiom**	I'm so hungry I could eat a horse. **Hyperbole**	The snake hissed as it slithered quickly through the grass. **Onomatopoeia**	The turn appeared as quick as a wink. **Simile**

Novel Review
Generating Questions

Directions: Copy a handout for each student. Students complete the starter phrases to write discussion questions for the current novel of study or chapter review. When completed, students use the Find Someone Who structure as a class review.

Novel Review Questions

What if…	Which character…	List the things that…
Do you agree…	What changes…	Did the conflict…
What is one example…	Did the main character…	How did the author…
Did the setting…	What is the difference…	How could you describe…

Parts of Speech

Directions: Copy a handout for each student. Students ask partners for an example of the part of speech listed from the current novel of study or chapter review. Students record their partner's response. Partners initial their response on the blank line.

Parts of Speech

Action verb	Common noun	Preposition	Adjective	Proper noun
Prepositional phrase	Adverb	Linking verb	Article	Helping verb
Pronoun	Coordinating conjunction	Interjection	Collective noun	Possessive noun
Compound noun	Adverb	Prepositional phrase	Action verb	Plural noun
Common noun	Adjective	Proper noun	Linking verb	Pronoun

• I Ask
• You Answer
• I Write
• You Initial

Find Someone Who
Blackline

Elements of a Novel or Story

Directions: Copy a handout for each student. Students ask partners for an example of an element from any novel or story and record their partner's response. Partners initial on the blank line.

Elements of a Novel or Story

Protagonist	Example of imagery	Antagonist	Resolution	Author
_____	_____	_____	_____	_____
Minor character	Setting: Time	Favorite part	Metaphor to describe the conflict	Main idea of plot
_____	_____	_____	_____	_____
How does the main character change?	Symbolism example	Setting: Place(s)	Another work by this author	Main character's traits
_____	_____	_____	_____	_____
Theme	Author's point of view	Would you recommend this book? Why?	High point in action	Conflict/ problem
_____	_____	_____	_____	_____

Vocabulary Builder

Directions: Copy a handout for each student. Students Find Someone Who can provide vocabulary words that begin with the letters in each box. Students should acquire several entries per letter. Students record words and their partner initials each entry.

Vocabulary Builder Worksheet

A B	C D	E F	G H

I J	K L	M N	O P

Q R	S T	U V W	X Y Z

• I Ask
• You Answer
• I Write
• You Initial

Find Someone Who
Blackline

Short Story Review
"To Build a Fire"

Directions: Copy a handout for each student. Students find someone who can provide one answer. Students record their partner's answer and the partner initials on the blank line.

Short Story Review Worksheet

Example of or your own simile from story	Character's goal	Main character(s)	Setting	Favorite part
Protagonist	Plot	Author of "To Build a Fire"	Problem	Another work by this author
Outcome of first fire	Example of imagery	Theme	Outcome of third fire	Minor character(s)
Turning Point	Outcome of second fire	Resolution	Antagonist	Author's point of view

Find Someone Who
Blank Worksheet Template

- I Ask
- You Answer
- I Write
- You Initial

Directions: Fill in a question or discussion prompt in each box below. Students use the form to get answers or ideas from classmates.

Topic:				
____	____	____	____	____
____	____	____	____	____
____	____	____	____	____
____	____	____	____	____

Mix-N-Match

Structure 3

Terra   Earth

Terra   Earth

Mix-N-Match

Students mix, repeatedly quizzing new partners and trading cards. Afterwards, they rush to find a partner with the card that matches theirs.

Group Size
Whole Class

Steps

Setup: Students each receive one card.

① Students Mix and Pair
With a card in one hand and the other hand raised, each student mixes around the room, looking for a partner with a raised hand. When they pair up, they give each other a high five. *"Pair up with another student with a raised hand. Give each other a high five and lower your hands."*

② Partner A Asks Question
In the pair, Partner A asks the other a question relating to his or her card. For example, *"What is an oxymoron?"*

③ Partner B Answers
Partner B answers Partner A's question. *"A phrase with words that contradict each other."*

④ Partner A Praises or Coaches
If Partner B answers correctly, Partner A praises him or her. *"That's right. Good definition."* If Partner B answers incorrectly, Partner A provides the correct answer and coaches or tutors Partner B.

⑤ Switch Roles
Partners switch roles. Partner B now asks the question and offers praise or coaches.

⑥ Partners Trade Cards
Before departing and looking for new partners, partners trade cards. This way, students have a new card for each new pairing.

⑦ Continue Quizzing and Trading
Partners split up and continue quizzing and getting quizzed by new partners. When done, they trade cards again and find a new partner.

⑧ Teacher Calls, "Freeze"
After a sufficient time of quizzing and trading cards elapses, the teacher calls, *"Freeze."* Students freeze, read their cards, and think of their match.

⑨ Find Match
The teacher calls, *"Match."* Students search for a classmate with the matching card. When they find each other, they move to the outside of the classroom so students still searching for a match can find each other more easily.

Activities

Tips

• Distribute cards sequence so for every student that has a question card, there is a student with a matching answer card.
• If there are an odd number of students, hold onto the last answer card so you may pair with a student and every question will have an answer.
• Determine who will go first in each pairing. For example, Partner A can always be the taller student or the student more colorfully dressed.
• Laminate cards for durability and future use.

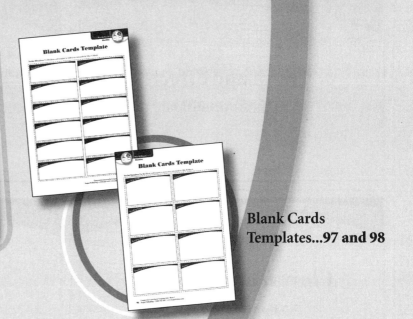

Blank Cards
Templates...**97 and 98**

Reading Terms

Directions: Cut out the cards on the dotted line. Give one card to each student. Distribute cards in sequence so for every student with a Reading Term card, there is a student with a matching Answer card.

Reading Term

Analysis

What is the definition?

Reading Terms

Answer

Definition: Process of breaking down something into its parts and examining a poem's rhyme, mood, imagery, and theme.

What is the reading term?

Reading Terms

Reading Term

Author's Purpose

What is the definition?

Reading Terms

Answer

Definition: To entertain the reader, explain or inform, express an opinion, or persuade reader to believe or do something.

What is the reading term?

Reading Terms

Reading Term

Cause and Effect

What is the definition?

Reading Terms

Answer

Definition: Relationship between events in a piece of literature. One event brings about the next event.

What is the reading term?

Reading Terms

Reading Term

Chronological Order

What is the definition?

Reading Terms

Answer

Definition: Sequence of events or order in which a plot develops.

What is the reading term?

Reading Terms

Reading Terms *(continued)*

Directions: Cut out the cards on the dotted line. Give one card to each student. Distribute cards in sequence so for every student with a Reading Term card, there is a student with a matching Answer card.

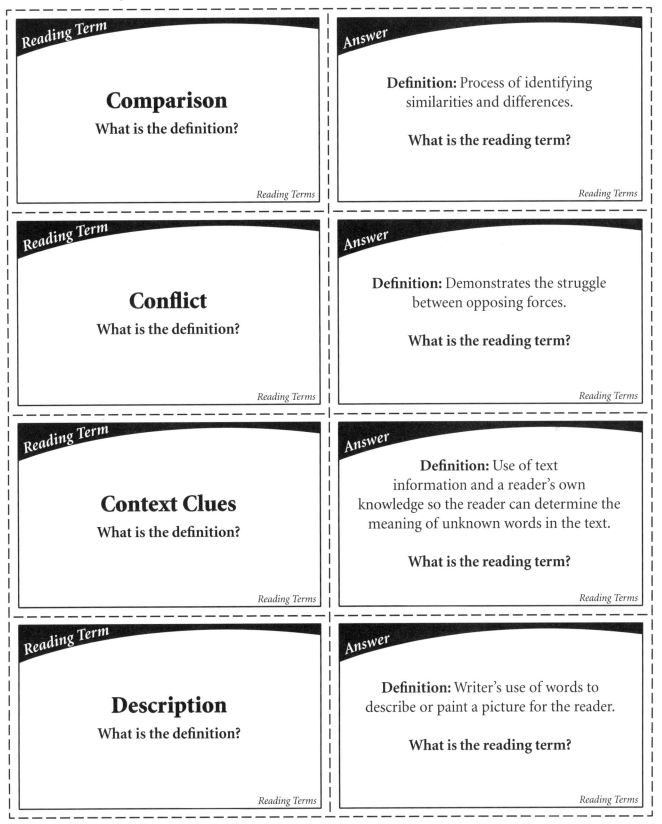

Reading Term

Comparison

What is the definition?

Reading Terms

Answer

Definition: Process of identifying similarities and differences.

What is the reading term?

Reading Terms

Reading Term

Conflict

What is the definition?

Reading Terms

Answer

Definition: Demonstrates the struggle between opposing forces.

What is the reading term?

Reading Terms

Reading Term

Context Clues

What is the definition?

Reading Terms

Answer

Definition: Use of text information and a reader's own knowledge so the reader can determine the meaning of unknown words in the text.

What is the reading term?

Reading Terms

Reading Term

Description

What is the definition?

Reading Terms

Answer

Definition: Writer's use of words to describe or paint a picture for the reader.

What is the reading term?

Reading Terms

Reading Terms (continued)

Directions: Cut out the cards on the dotted line. Give one card to each student. Distribute cards in sequence so for every student with a Reading Term card, there is a student with a matching Answer card.

Reading Term

Exaggeration

What is the definition?

Reading Terms

Answer

Definition: Statement intimating that something means much more than it actually says.

What is the reading term?

Reading Terms

Reading Term

Exposition

What is the definition?

Reading Terms

Answer

Definition: Writer laying the foundation by using prior knowledge to introduce the story.

What is the reading term?

Reading Terms

Reading Term

Fact and Opinion

What is the definition?

Reading Terms

Answer

Definition: Statement that can or cannot be proven, may reflect personal beliefs, and may often be debatable.

What is the reading term?

Reading Terms

Reading Term

Inference

What is the definition?

Reading Terms

Answer

Definition: Logical guess or conclusion based on evidence that allows a reader to figure out more than the words can say.

What is the reading term?

Reading Terms

Reading Terms (continued)

Directions: Cut out the cards on the dotted line. Give one card to each student. Distribute cards in sequence so for every student with a Reading Term card, there is a student with a matching Answer card.

Reading Term

Main Idea

What is the definition?

Reading Terms

Answer

Definition: Point an author is making about a topic.

What is the reading term?

Reading Terms

Reading Term

Persuasion

What is the definition?

Reading Terms

Answer

Definition: Type of reading or writing meant to sway the reader's feelings, beliefs, or actions.

What is the reading term?

Reading Terms

Reading Term

Prior Knowledge

What is the definition?

Reading Terms

Answer

Definition: The knowledge a reader has prior to reading the material allows readers to connect what they are learning with what they already know.

What is the reading term?

Reading Terms

Reading Term

Questioning

What is the definition?

Reading Terms

Answer

Definition: Process of raising questions while reading.

What is the reading term?

Reading Terms

Reading Terms (continued)

Directions: Cut out the cards on the dotted line. Give one card to each student. Distribute cards in sequence so for every student with a Reading Term card, there is a student with a matching Answer card.

Reading Term

Setting

What is the definition?

Reading Terms

Answer

Definition: Time and place of the action in the story or play.

What is the reading term?

Reading Terms

Reading Term

Symbol

What is the definition?

Reading Terms

Answer

Definition: Person, place, or object that represents something beyond itself.

What is the reading term?

Reading Terms

Reading Term

Synthesize

What is the definition?

Reading Terms

Answer

Definition: To combine two separate ideas into one new idea.

What is the reading term?

Reading Terms

Reading Term

Theme

What is the definition?

Reading Terms

Answer

Definition: Message the story conveys in a novel or short story.

What is the reading term?

Reading Terms

Reading Terms and Definitions

Directions: Use this resource page to introduce students to reading terms and their meanings and/or to check answers.

- **Analysis**—Process of breaking down something into its parts and examining a poem's rhyme, mood, imagery, and theme.

- **Author's Purpose**—To entertain the reader, explain or inform, express an opinion, or persuade reader to believe or do something.

- **Cause and Effect**—Relationship between events in a piece of literature. One event brings about the next event.

- **Chronological Order**—Sequence of events or order in which a plot develops.

- **Comparison**—Process of identifying similarities and differences.

- **Conflict**—Demonstrates the struggle between opposing forces.

- **Context Clues**—Use of text information and a reader's own knowledge so the reader can determine the meaning of unknown words in the text.

- **Description**—Writer's use of words to describe or paint a picture for the reader.

- **Exaggeration**—Statement intimating that something means much more than it actually says.

- **Exposition**—Writer laying the foundation by using prior knowledge to introduce the story.

- **Fact and Opinion**—Statement that can or cannot be proven, may reflect personal beliefs, and may often be debatable.

- **Inference**—Logical guess or conclusion based on evidence that allows a reader to figure out more than the words can say.

- **Main Idea**—Point an author is making about a topic.

- **Persuasion**—Type of reading or writing meant to sway the reader's feelings, beliefs, or actions.

- **Prior Knowledge**—The knowledge a reader has prior to reading the material allows readers to connect what they are learning with what they already know.

- **Questioning**—Process of raising questions while reading.

- **Setting**—Time and place of the action in the story or play.

- **Symbol**—Person, place, or object that represents something beyond itself.

- **Synthesize**—To combine two separate ideas into one new idea.

- **Theme**—Message the story conveys in a novel or short story.

Root Words

Directions: Give one card to each student. Distribute cards in sequence so for every student with a Word card, there is a student with a matching Root Word card.

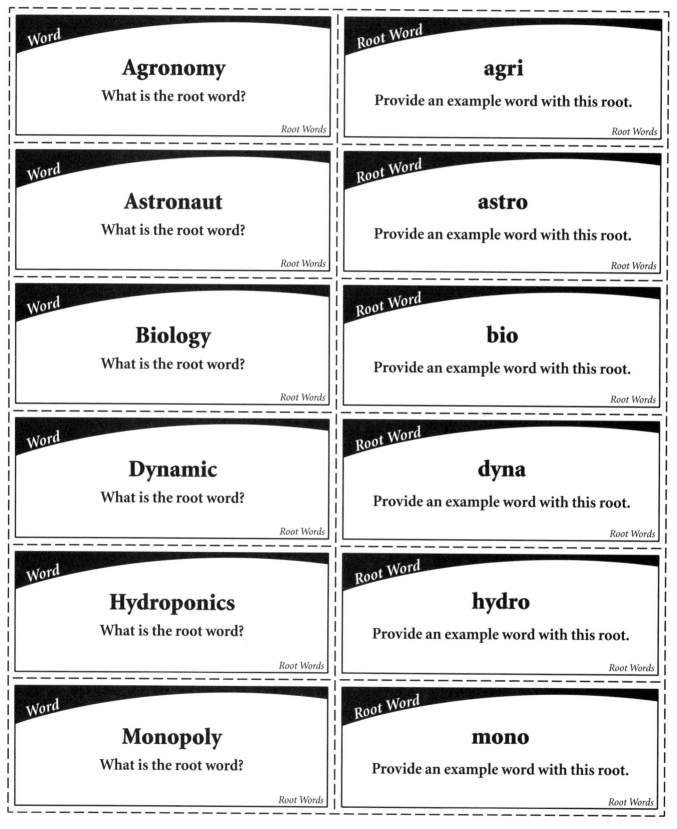

Word

Agronomy

What is the root word?

Root Words

Root Word

agri

Provide an example word with this root.

Root Words

Word

Astronaut

What is the root word?

Root Words

Root Word

astro

Provide an example word with this root.

Root Words

Word

Biology

What is the root word?

Root Words

Root Word

bio

Provide an example word with this root.

Root Words

Word

Dynamic

What is the root word?

Root Words

Root Word

dyna

Provide an example word with this root.

Root Words

Word

Hydroponics

What is the root word?

Root Words

Root Word

hydro

Provide an example word with this root.

Root Words

Word

Monopoly

What is the root word?

Root Words

Root Word

mono

Provide an example word with this root.

Root Words

Root Words (continued)

Directions: Give one card to each student. Distribute cards in sequence so for every student with a Word card, there is a student with a matching Root Word card.

Word

Orthodox

What is the root word?

Root Words

Root Word

ortho

Provide an example word with this root.

Root Words

Word

Heliotrope

What is the root word?

Root Words

Root Word

helio

Provide an example word with this root.

Root Words

Word

Precede

What is the root word?

Root Words

Root Word

cede

Provide an example word with this root.

Root Words

Word

Epidermis

What is the root word?

Root Words

Root Word

derma

Provide an example word with this root.

Root Words

Word

Multimillionaire

What is the root word?

Root Words

Root Word

multi

Provide an example word with this root.

Root Words

Word

Manuscript

What is the root word?

Root Words

Root Word

script

Provide an example word with this root.

Root Words

Root Words (continued)

Directions: Give one card to each student. Distribute cards in sequence so for every student with a Word card, there is a student with a matching Root Word card.

Word **Terrace** What is the root word? *Root Words*	**Root Word** **terra** Provide an example word with this root. *Root Words*
Word **Thermometer** What is the root word? *Root Words*	**Root Word** **thermo** Provide an example word with this root. *Root Words*
Word **Democracy** What is the root word? *Root Words*	**Root Word** **demo** Provide an example word with this root. *Root Words*
Word **Autograph** What is the root word? *Root Words*	**Root Word** **graph** Provide an example word with this root. *Root Words*
Word **Automobile** What is the root word? *Root Words*	**Root Word** **auto** Provide an example word with this root. *Root Words*
Word **Transmit** What is the root word? *Root Words*	**Root Word** **trans** Provide an example word with this root. *Root Words*

Root Words (continued)

Directions: Give one card to each student. Distribute cards in sequence so for every student with a Word card, there is a student with a matching Root Word card.

Word	Root Word
Spectator What is the root word? *Root Words*	**spect** Provide an example word with this root. *Root Words*
Television What is the root word? *Root Words*	**tele** Provide an example word with this root. *Root Words*
Synthesis What is the root word? *Root Words*	**syn** Provide an example word with this root. *Root Words*
Equilateral What is the root word? *Root Words*	**equi** Provide an example word with this root. *Root Words*
Triangle What is the root word? *Root Words*	**tri** Provide an example word with this root. *Root Words*
Vitamin What is the root word? *Root Words*	**vita** Provide an example word with this root. *Root Words*

Root Words *(continued)*

Directions: Give one card to each student. Distribute cards in sequence so for every student with a Word card, there is a student with a matching Root Word card.

Word **Paramedic** What is the root word? *Root Words*	**Root Word** **para** Provide an example word with this root. *Root Words*
Word **Hypersensitive** What is the root word? *Root Words*	**Root Word** **hyper** Provide an example word with this root. *Root Words*
Word **Megalopolis** What is the root word? *Root Words*	**Root Word** **mega** Provide an example word with this root. *Root Words*
Word **Metamorphosis** What is the root word? *Root Words*	**Root Word** **meta** Provide an example word with this root. *Root Words*
Word **Flexible** What is the root word? *Root Words*	**Root Word** **flex** Provide an example word with this root. *Root Words*
Word **Periscope** What is the root word? *Root Words*	**Root Word** **peri** Provide an example word with this root. *Root Words*

Root Words and Meanings

Directions: Give one card to each student. Distribute cards in sequence so for every student with a Root Word card, there is a student with a matching Meaning card.

Root Word

agri

What is its meaning?

Root Words and Meanings

Meaning

Meaning: field

What is the root word?

Root Words and Meanings

Root Word

astro

What is its meaning?

Root Words and Meanings

Meaning

Meaning: star

What is the root word?

Root Words and Meanings

Root Word

bio

What is its meaning?

Root Words and Meanings

Meaning

Meaning: life

What is the root word?

Root Words and Meanings

Root Word

dyna

What is its meaning?

Root Words and Meanings

Meaning

Meaning: power

What is the root word?

Root Words and Meanings

Root Word

hydro

What is its meaning?

Root Words and Meanings

Meaning

Meaning: water

What is the root word?

Root Words and Meanings

Root Word

mono

What is its meaning?

Root Words and Meanings

Meaning

Meaning: one

What is the root word?

Root Words and Meanings

Root Words and Meanings (continued)

Directions: Give one card to each student. Distribute cards in sequence so for every student with a Root Word card, there is a student with a matching Meaning card.

Root Word	Meaning
ortho What is its meaning? *Root Words and Meanings*	**Meaning:** straight What is the root word? *Root Words and Meanings*
helio What is its meaning? *Root Words and Meanings*	**Meaning:** sun What is the root word? *Root Words and Meanings*
cede What is its meaning? *Root Words and Meanings*	**Meaning:** go What is the root word? *Root Words and Meanings*
derma What is its meaning? *Root Words and Meanings*	**Meaning:** skin What is the root word? *Root Words and Meanings*
multi What is its meaning? *Root Words and Meanings*	**Meaning:** many What is the root word? *Root Words and Meanings*
script What is its meaning? *Root Words and Meanings*	**Meaning:** write What is the root word? *Root Words and Meanings*

Root Words and Meanings *(continued)*

Directions: Give one card to each student. Distribute cards in sequence so for every student with a Root Word card, there is a student with a matching Meaning card.

Root Word	Meaning
terra What is its meaning? *Root Words and Meanings*	**Meaning:** earth What is the root word? *Root Words and Meanings*
thermo What is its meaning? *Root Words and Meanings*	**Meaning:** heat What is the root word? *Root Words and Meanings*
demo What is its meaning? *Root Words and Meanings*	**Meaning:** people What is the root word? *Root Words and Meanings*
graph What is its meaning? *Root Words and Meanings*	**Meaning:** write What is the root word? *Root Words and Meanings*
auto What is its meaning? *Root Words and Meanings*	**Meaning:** self What is the root word? *Root Words and Meanings*
trans What is its meaning? *Root Words and Meanings*	**Meaning:** across What is the root word? *Root Words and Meanings*

Root Words and Meanings *(continued)*

Directions: Give one card to each student. Distribute cards in sequence so for every student with a Root Word card, there is a student with a matching Meaning card.

Root Word

spect

What is its meaning?

Root Words and Meanings

Meaning

Meaning: to look

What is the root word?

Root Words and Meanings

Root Word

tele

What is its meaning?

Root Words and Meanings

Meaning

Meaning: far away

What is the root word?

Root Words and Meanings

Root Word

syn

What is its meaning?

Root Words and Meanings

Meaning

Meaning: same or together

What is the root word?

Root Words and Meanings

Root Word

equi

What is its meaning?

Root Words and Meanings

Meaning

Meaning: equal

What is the root word?

Root Words and Meanings

Root Word

tri

What is its meaning?

Root Words and Meanings

Meaning

Meaning: three

What is the root word?

Root Words and Meanings

Root Word

vita

What is its meaning?

Root Words and Meanings

Meaning

Meaning: life

What is the root word?

Root Words and Meanings

Root Words and Meanings *(continued)*

Directions: Give one card to each student. Distribute cards in sequence so for every student with a Root Word card, there is a student with a matching Meaning card.

Root Word	Meaning
para What is its meaning? *Root Words and Meanings*	Meaning: beside What is the root word? *Root Words and Meanings*
hyper What is its meaning? *Root Words and Meanings*	Meaning: over or above What is the root word? *Root Words and Meanings*
mega What is its meaning? *Root Words and Meanings*	Meaning: great or million What is the root word? *Root Words and Meanings*
meta What is its meaning? *Root Words and Meanings*	Meaning: beyond or change What is the root word? *Root Words and Meanings*
flex What is its meaning? *Root Words and Meanings*	Meaning: to bend What is the root word? *Root Words and Meanings*
peri What is its meaning? *Root Words and Meanings*	Meaning: around What is the root word? *Root Words and Meanings*

Root Words and Meanings

Directions: Use this resource page to introduce students to root words and their meanings and/or to check answers.

- **multi**—many
  Example: Multimillionaire

- **equi**—equal
  Example: Equilateral

- **agri**—field
  Example: Agronomy

- **script**—write
  Example: Manuscript

- **tri**—three
  Example: Triangle

- **astro**—star
  Example: Astronaut

- **terra**—earth
  Example: Terrace

- **vita**—life
  Example: Vitamin

- **bio**—life
  Example: Biology

- **thermo**—heat
  Example: Thermometer

- **para**—beside
  Example: Paramedic

- **dyna**—power
  Example: Dynamic

- **demo**—people
  Example: Democracy

- **hyper**—over or above
  Example: Hypersensitive

- **hydro**—water
  Example: Hydroponics

- **graph**—write
  Example: Autograph

- **mega**—great or million
  Example: Megalopolis

- **mono**—one
  Example: Monopoly

- **auto**—self
  Example: Automobile

- **meta**—beyond or change
  Example: Metamorphosis

- **ortho**—straight
  Example: Orthodox

- **trans**—across
  Example: Transmit

- **flex**—to bend
  Example: Flexible

- **helio**—sun
  Example: Heliotrope

- **spect**—to look
  Example: Spectator

- **peri**—around
  Example: Periscope

- **cede**—go
  Example: Precede

- **tele**—far away
  Example: Television

- **derma**—skin
  Example: Epidermis

- **syn**—same or together
  Example: Synthesis

Similes

Directions: Give one card to each student. Distribute cards in sequence so for every student with a Simile card, there is a student with a matching Meaning card. When students ask for the simile, they may use the hint provided if necessary.

Simile	Meaning
As dry as a bone. What does it mean? *Similes*	**Meaning:** Something that is very dry or boring such as a lecture. **What is the simile?** *Hint: Dry* *Similes*
As easy as apple pie. What does it mean? *Similes*	**Meaning:** Something simple or easy to do. **What is the simile?** *Hint: Easy* *Similes*
As fit as a fiddle. What does it mean? *Similes*	**Meaning:** Being in good condition or physical shape. **What is the simile?** *Hint: Fit* *Similes*
As gentle as a lamb. What does it mean? *Similes*	**Meaning:** To handle something very gently or carefully. **What is the simile?** *Hint: Gentle* *Similes*
As pleased as punch. What does it mean? *Similes*	**Meaning:** To be very proud of someone or something. **What is the simile?** *Hint: Pleased* *Similes*
As slippery as an eel. What does it mean? *Similes*	**Meaning:** Evasive, not to be trusted. **What is the simile?** *Hint: Slippery* *Similes*

Similes (continued)

Directions: Give one card to each student. Distribute cards in sequence so for every student with a Simile card, there is a student with a matching Meaning card. When students ask for the simile, they may use the hint provided if necessary.

Simile	Meaning
As smooth as silk. **What does it mean?** *Similes*	**Meaning:** Smooth to the touch, or something that is easy to do. **What is the simile?** *Hint: Silk* *Similes*
As stubborn as a mule. **What does it mean?** *Similes*	**Meaning:** To be obstinate or very stubborn. **What is the simile?** *Hint: Mule* *Similes*
As thick as thieves. **What does it mean?** *Similes*	**Meaning:** Very good or best of friends; enjoy being together. **What is the simile?** *Hint: Thieves* *Similes*
As wise as an owl. **What does it mean?** *Similes*	**Meaning:** Intelligent, rather wise. **What is the simile?** *Hint: Owl* *Similes*
As delicate as a flower. **What does it mean?** *Similes*	**Meaning:** Someone or something that is fragile or easily broken. **What is the simile?** *Hint: Flower* *Similes*
As bright as the sun. **What does it mean?** *Similes*	**Meaning:** Someone or something that is bright and cheery. **What is the simile?** *Hint: Sun* *Similes*

Similes (continued)

Directions: Give one card to each student. Distribute cards in sequence so for every student with a Simile card, there is a student with a matching Meaning card. When students ask for the simile, they may use the hint provided if necessary.

Simile	Meaning
As cool as a cucumber. **What does it mean?** _{Similes}	**Meaning:** Someone who can handle situations without stress. **What is the simile?** *Hint: Cucumber* _{Similes}
As fresh as a daisy. **What does it mean?** _{Similes}	**Meaning:** Clean looking or smelling. **What is the simile?** *Hint: Daisy* _{Similes}
As good as gold. **What does it mean?** _{Similes}	**Meaning:** Someone who is obedient and follows the rules. **What is the simile?** *Hint: Gold* _{Similes}
As black as coal. **What does it mean?** _{Similes}	**Meaning:** Solid black in color. **What is the simile?** *Hint: Coal* _{Similes}
As clear as a bell. **What does it mean?** _{Similes}	**Meaning:** Sharp, clear, and to the point. **What is the simile?** *Hint: Bell* _{Similes}
As neat as a pin. **What does it mean?** _{Similes}	**Meaning:** Someone who is tidy and organized. **What is the simile?** *Hint: Pin* _{Similes}

Similes (continued)

Directions: Give one card to each student. Distribute cards in sequence so for every student with a Simile card, there is a student with a matching Meaning card. When students ask for the simile, they may use the hint provided if necessary.

Simile	Meaning
As tough as leather. **What does it mean?** *Similes*	**Meaning:** Very strong and tough. **What is the simile?** *Hint: Leather* *Similes*
As white as snow. **What does it mean?** *Similes*	**Meaning:** Pure white. **What is the simile?** *Hint: White* *Similes*
As snug as a bug in a rug. **What does it mean?** *Similes*	**Meaning:** Comfortable spot or position. **What is the simile?** *Hint: Bug* *Similes*
As quiet as a mouse. **What does it mean?** *Similes*	**Meaning:** Being still, very quiet, not being noticed. **What is the simile?** *Hint: Mouse* *Similes*
As pure as the driven snow. **What does it mean?** *Similes*	**Meaning:** Pure and innocent. **What is the simile?** *Hint: Snow* *Similes*
As sure as death and taxes. **What does it mean?** *Similes*	**Meaning:** Something that is absolutely certain to happen. **What is the simile?** *Hint: Death* *Similes*

Similes *(continued)*

Directions: Give one card to each student. Distribute cards in sequence so for every student with a Simile card, there is a student with a matching Meaning card. When students ask for the simile, they may use the hint provided if necessary.

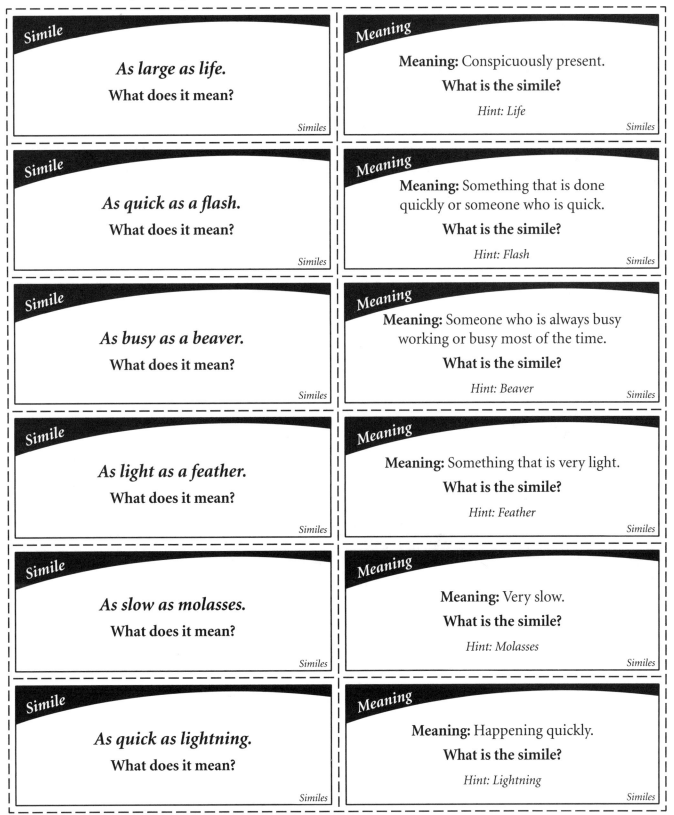

Simile	Meaning
As large as life. What does it mean? *Similes*	**Meaning:** Conspicuously present. **What is the simile?** *Hint: Life* *Similes*
As quick as a flash. What does it mean? *Similes*	**Meaning:** Something that is done quickly or someone who is quick. **What is the simile?** *Hint: Flash* *Similes*
As busy as a beaver. What does it mean? *Similes*	**Meaning:** Someone who is always busy working or busy most of the time. **What is the simile?** *Hint: Beaver* *Similes*
As light as a feather. What does it mean? *Similes*	**Meaning:** Something that is very light. **What is the simile?** *Hint: Feather* *Similes*
As slow as molasses. What does it mean? *Similes*	**Meaning:** Very slow. **What is the simile?** *Hint: Molasses* *Similes*
As quick as lightning. What does it mean? *Similes*	**Meaning:** Happening quickly. **What is the simile?** *Hint: Lightning* *Similes*

Similes (continued)

Directions: Give one card to each student. Distribute cards in sequence so for every student with a Simile card, there is a student with a matching Meaning card. When students ask for the simile, they may use the hint provided if necessary.

Simile	Meaning
As hungry as a wolf. **What does it mean?** *Similes*	**Meaning:** Someone who says they are very hungry. **What is the simile?** *Hint: Wolf* *Similes*
As thin as a rail. **What does it mean?** *Similes*	**Meaning:** Very thin, quite skinny. **What is the simile?** *Hint: Rail* *Similes*
As white as a ghost. **What does it mean?** *Similes*	**Meaning:** Looking scared. **What is the simile?** *Hint: Ghost* *Similes*
As poor as a church mouse. **What does it mean?** *Similes*	**Meaning:** So poor you are living in poverty. **What is the simile?** *Hint: Church* *Similes*
Simile *Similes*	Meaning *Similes*
Simile *Similes*	Meaning *Similes*

Similes and Meanings

Directions: Use this resource page to introduce students to similes and their meanings and/or to check answers.

- **As dry as a bone**—Something that is very dry or boring such as a lecture.

- **As easy as apple pie**—Something simple or easy to do.

- **As fit as a fiddle**—Being in good condition or physical shape.

- **As gentle as a lamb**—To handle something very gently or carefully.

- **As pleased as punch**—To be very proud of someone or something.

- **As slippery as an eel**—Evasive, not to be trusted.

- **As smooth as silk**—Smooth to the touch, or something that is easy to do.

- **As stubborn as a mule**—To be obstinate or very stubborn.

- **As thick as thieves**—Very good or best of friends; enjoy being together.

- **As wise as an owl**—Intelligent, rather wise.

- **As delicate as a flower**—Someone or something that is fragile or easily broken.

- **As bright as the sun**—Someone or something that is bright and cheery.

- **As cool as a cucumber**—Someone who can handle situations without stress.

- **As fresh as a daisy**—Clean looking or smelling.

- **As good as gold**—Someone who is obedient and follows the rules.

- **As black as coal**—Solid black in color.

- **As clear as a bell**—Sharp, clear, and to the point.

- **As neat as a pin**—Someone who is tidy and organized.

- **As tough as leather**—Very strong and tough.

- **As white as snow**—Pure white.

- **As snug as a bug in a rug**—Comfortable spot or position.

- **As quiet as a mouse**—Being still, very quiet, not being noticed.

- **As pure as the driven snow**—Pure and innocent.

- **As sure as death and taxes**—Something that is absolutely certain to happen.

- **As large as life**—Conspicuously present.

- **As quick as a flash**—Something that is done quickly or someone who is quick.

- **As busy as a beaver**—Someone who is always busy working or busy most of the time.

- **As light as a feather**—Something that is very light.

- **As slow as molasses**—Very slow.

- **As quick as lightning**—Happening quickly.

- **As hungry as a wolf**—Someone who says they are very hungry.

- **As thin as a rail**—Very thin, quite skinny.

- **As white as a ghost**—Looking scared.

- **As poor as a church mouse**—So poor you are living in poverty.

Prefixes and Suffixes

Directions: Give one card to each student. Distribute cards in sequence so for every student with a Prefix or Suffix card, there is a student with a matching Meaning card.

Prefix	Meaning
Unfriendly What is its prefix? What does the prefix mean? *Prefixes and Suffixes*	**Prefix Meaning:** not What is the prefix? What is an example? *Prefixes and Suffixes*
Overdo What is its prefix? What does the prefix mean? *Prefixes and Suffixes*	**Prefix Meaning:** on top; excessive What is the prefix? What is an example? *Prefixes and Suffixes*
Unabridged What is its prefix? What does the prefix mean? *Prefixes and Suffixes*	**Prefix Meaning:** reverse of What is the prefix? What is an example? *Prefixes and Suffixes*
Submerge What is its prefix? What does the prefix mean? *Prefixes and Suffixes*	**Prefix Meaning:** under or beneath What is the prefix? What is an example? *Prefixes and Suffixes*
Encourage What is its prefix? What does the prefix mean? *Prefixes and Suffixes*	**Prefix Meaning:** in What is the prefix? What is an example? *Prefixes and Suffixes*
Interact What is its prefix? What does the prefix mean? *Prefixes and Suffixes*	**Prefix Meaning:** among or between What is the prefix? What is an example? *Prefixes and Suffixes*

Prefixes and Suffixes (continued)

Directions: Give one card to each student. Distribute cards in sequence so for every student with a Prefix or Suffix card, there is a student with a matching Meaning card.

Prefix
Disconnect
What is its prefix?
What does the prefix mean?
Prefixes and Suffixes

Meaning
Prefix Meaning: absence of
What is the prefix?
What is an example?
Prefixes and Suffixes

Prefix
Postwar
What is its prefix?
What does the prefix mean?
Prefixes and Suffixes

Meaning
Prefix Meaning: after
What is the prefix?
What is an example?
Prefixes and Suffixes

Prefix
Synonym
What is its prefix?
What does the prefix mean?
Prefixes and Suffixes

Meaning
Prefix Meaning: together
What is the prefix?
What is an example?
Prefixes and Suffixes

Prefix
Mislead
What is its prefix?
What does the prefix mean?
Prefixes and Suffixes

Meaning
Prefix Meaning: wrong
What is the prefix?
What is an example?
Prefixes and Suffixes

Suffix
Careful
What is its suffix?
What does the suffix mean?
Prefixes and Suffixes

Meaning
Suffix Meaning: full of
What is the suffix?
What is an example?
Prefixes and Suffixes

Suffix
Tasteless
What is its suffix?
What does the suffix mean?
Prefixes and Suffixes

Meaning
Suffix Meaning: without
What is the suffix?
What is an example?
Prefixes and Suffixes

Prefixes and Suffixes (continued)

Directions: Give one card to each student. Distribute cards in sequence so for every student with a Prefix or Suffix card, there is a student with a matching Meaning card.

Suffix

Pianist

What is its suffix?
What does the suffix mean?

Prefixes and Suffixes

Meaning

Suffix Meaning: one who is

What is the suffix?
What is an example?

Prefixes and Suffixes

Suffix

Patiently

What is its suffix?
What does the suffix mean?

Prefixes and Suffixes

Meaning

Suffix Meaning: characteristic of

What is the suffix?
What is an example?

Prefixes and Suffixes

Suffix

Kindness

What is its suffix?
What does the suffix mean?

Prefixes and Suffixes

Meaning

Suffix Meaning: a condition of

What is the suffix?
What is an example?

Prefixes and Suffixes

Suffix

Portable

What is its suffix?
What does the suffix mean?

Prefixes and Suffixes

Meaning

Suffix Meaning: able to be carried

What is the suffix?
What is an example?

Prefixes and Suffixes

Suffix

Boxes

What is its suffix?
What does the suffix mean?

Prefixes and Suffixes

Meaning

Suffix Meaning: more than one

What is the suffix?
What is an example?

Prefixes and Suffixes

Suffix

Illustrator

What is its suffix?
What does the suffix mean?

Prefixes and Suffixes

Meaning

Suffix Meaning: one who is

What is the suffix?
What is an example?

Prefixes and Suffixes

Prefixes and Suffixes (continued)

Directions: Give one card to each student. Distribute cards in sequence so for every student with a Prefix or Suffix card, there is a student with a matching Meaning card.

Suffix	Meaning
Enforcement **What is its suffix?** **What does the suffix mean?** *Prefixes and Suffixes*	**Meaning:** an action or process **What is the suffix?** **What is an example?** *Prefixes and Suffixes*

Suffix	Meaning
Beautician **What is its suffix?** **What does the suffix mean?** *Prefixes and Suffixes*	**Meaning:** one who practices **What is the suffix?** **What is an example?** *Prefixes and Suffixes*

Prefix	Meaning
Prefixes and Suffixes	*Prefixes and Suffixes*

Prefix	Meaning
Prefixes and Suffixes	*Prefixes and Suffixes*

Suffix	Meaning
Prefixes and Suffixes	*Prefixes and Suffixes*

Suffix	Meaning
Prefixes and Suffixes	*Prefixes and Suffixes*

Prefixes, Suffixes, and Meanings

Directions: Use this resource page to introduce students to prefixes, suffixes, and their meanings and/or to check answers.

Prefixes:

- **Un**—not
  Example: Unfriendly

- **Over**—on top; excessive
  Example: Overdo

- **Un**—reverse of
  Example: Unabridged

- **Sub**—under or beneath
  Example: Submerge

- **En**—in
  Example: Encourage

- **Inter**—among or between
  Example: Interact

- **Dis**—absence of
  Example: Disconnect

- **Post**—after
  Example: Postwar

- **Syn**—together
  Example: Synonym

- **Mis**—wrong
  Example: Mislead

Suffixes:

- **ful**—full of
  Example: Careful

- **less**—without
  Example: Tasteless

- **ist**—one who is
  Example: Pianist

- **ly**—characteristic of
  Example: Patiently

- **ness**—a condition of
  Example: Kindness

- **able**—able to be carried
  Example: Portable

- **es**—more than one
  Example: Boxes

- **or**—one who is
  Example: Illustrator

- **ment**—an action or process
  Example: Enforcement

- **ian**—one who practices
  Example: Beautician

Prefixes

Directions: Cut out cards along the dotted line. Give one card to each student. Distribute cads in sequence so for every student with a Prefix card, there is a student with a matching Meaning card.

Prefix
Preliminary, Previous
What prefix do these words begin with?
What does that prefix mean?
Prefixes

Meaning
Before
What prefix means *before*?
Give an example of this prefix.
Prefixes

Prefix
Postpone, Postoperative
What prefix do these words begin with?
What does that prefix mean?
Prefixes

Meaning
After
What prefix means *after*?
Give an example of this prefix.
Prefixes

Prefix
Intramural, Intravenous
What prefix do these words begin with?
What does that prefix mean?
Prefixes

Meaning
Within
What prefix means *within*?
Give an example of this prefix.
Prefixes

Prefix
Antecedent, Antebellum
What prefix do these words begin with?
What does that prefix mean?
Prefixes

Meaning
Before
What prefix means *before*?
Give an example of this prefix.
Prefixes

Prefix
Interstate, Interfere
What prefix do these words begin with?
What does that prefix mean?
Prefixes

Meaning
Between
What prefix means *between*?
Give an example of this prefix.
Prefixes

Prefix
Transport, Transaction
What prefix do these words begin with?
What does that prefix mean?
Prefixes

Meaning
Across
What prefix means *across*?
Give an example of this prefix.
Prefixes

Prefixes (continued)

Directions: Cut out cards along the dotted line. Give one card to each student. Distribute cads in sequence so for every student with a Prefix card, there is a student with a matching Meaning card.

Prefix

Submarine, Submerge

What prefix do these words begin with?
What does that prefix mean?

Prefixes

Meaning

Under

What prefix means *under*?
Give an example of this prefix.

Prefixes

Prefix

Circumference, Circumnavigate

What prefix do these words begin with?
What does that prefix mean?

Prefixes

Meaning

Around

What prefix means *around*?
Give an example of this prefix.

Prefixes

Prefix

Ultrasonic, Ultraconservative

What prefix do these words begin with?
What does that prefix mean?

Prefixes

Meaning

Excessive

What prefix means *excessive*?
Give an example of this prefix.

Prefixes

Prefix

Rearrange, Remake

What prefix do these words begin with?
What does that prefix mean?

Prefixes

Meaning

Again

What prefix means *again*?
Give an example of this prefix.

Prefixes

Prefix

Coauthor, Coeditor

What prefix do these words begin with?
What does that prefix mean?

Prefixes

Meaning

Together

What prefix means *together*?
Give an example of this prefix.

Prefixes

Prefix

Disbelief, Disrespect

What prefix do these words begin with?
What does that prefix mean?

Prefixes

Meaning

Not or not any

What prefix means *not* or *not any*?
Give an example of this prefix.

Prefixes

Prefixes *(continued)*

Directions: Cut out cards along the dotted line. Give one card to each student. Distribute cads in sequence so for every student with a Prefix card, there is a student with a matching Meaning card.

Prefix	Meaning
Nonessential, Nonviolence What prefix do these words begin with? What does that prefix mean? *Prefixes*	***Not*** What prefix means *not*? Give an example of this prefix. *Prefixes*
Deactivate, Decompress What prefix do these words begin with? What does that prefix mean? *Prefixes*	***Away*** or ***off*** What prefix means *away* or *off*? Give an example of this prefix. *Prefixes*
Extraordinary, Extraterrestrial What prefix do these words begin with? What does that prefix mean? *Prefixes*	***Outside*** or ***additional*** What prefix means *outside* or *additional*? Give an example of this prefix. *Prefixes*
Autoimmune, Autograph What prefix do these words begin with? What does that prefix mean? *Prefixes*	***Self*** What prefix means *self*? Give an example of this prefix. *Prefixes*
Decade, Decathlon What prefix do these words begin with? What does that prefix mean? *Prefixes*	***Ten*** What prefix means *ten*? Give an example of this prefix. *Prefixes*
Macroeconomics, Macrocosm What prefix do these words begin with? What does that prefix mean? *Prefixes*	***Large*** What prefix means *large*? Give an example of this prefix. *Prefixes*

Prefixes (continued)

Directions: Cut out cards along the dotted line. Give one card to each student. Distribute cads in sequence so for every student with a Prefix card, there is a student with a matching Meaning card.

Prefix

Periodontal, Periscope

What prefix do these words begin with?
What does that prefix mean?

Prefixes

Meaning

All around

What prefix means *all around*?
Give an example of this prefix.

Prefixes

Prefix

Anticlimax, Antiseptic

What prefix do these words begin with?
What does that prefix mean?

Prefixes

Meaning

Against

What prefix means *against*?
Give an example of this prefix.

Prefixes

Prefix

Monopoly, Monotheism

What prefix do these words begin with?
What does that prefix mean?

Prefixes

Meaning

Single

What prefix means *single*?
Give an example of this prefix.

Prefixes

Prefix

Symmetry, Symphony

What prefix do these words begin with?
What does that prefix mean?

Prefixes

Meaning

Together

What prefix means *together*?
Give an example of this prefix.

Prefixes

Prefix

Microscope, Microchip

What prefix do these words begin with?
What does that prefix mean?

Prefixes

Meaning

Small

What prefix means *small*?
Give an example of this prefix.

Prefixes

Prefix

Pseudonym, Pseudoscience

What prefix do these words begin with?
What does that prefix mean?

Prefixes

Meaning

False or *counterfeit*

What prefix means *false* or *counterfeit*?
Give an example of this prefix.

Prefixes

Prefixes *(continued)*

Directions: Cut out cards along the dotted line. Give one card to each student. Distribute cads in sequence so for every student with a Prefix card, there is a student with a matching Meaning card.

Prefix

Polygon, Polygamy

What prefix do these words begin with?
What does that prefix mean?

Prefixes

Meaning

Many

What prefix means *many*?
Give an example of this prefix.

Prefixes

Prefix

Misconception, Mistake

What prefix do these words begin with?
What does that prefix mean?

Prefixes

Meaning

Bad or *wrong*

What prefix means *bad* or *wrong*?
Give an example of this prefix.

Prefixes

Prefix

Unfounded, Unable

What prefix do these words begin with?
What does that prefix mean?

Prefixes

Meaning

Not

What prefix means *not*?
Give an example of this prefix.

Prefixes

Prefix

Benefactor, Benign

What prefix do these words begin with?
What does that prefix mean?

Prefixes

Meaning

Well or *good*

What prefix means *well* or *good*?
Give an example of this prefix.

Prefixes

Prefix

Adept, Admit

What prefix do these words begin with?
What does that prefix mean?

Prefixes

Meaning

To

What prefix means *to*?
Give an example of this prefix.

Prefixes

Prefix

Abandon, Abstain

What prefix do these words begin with?
What does that prefix mean?

Prefixes

Meaning

Away from or *off*

What prefix means *away from* or *off*?
Give an example of this prefix.

Prefixes

Synonyms

Directions: Cut out cards on dotted line. Give one card to each student. Distribute cards in sequence so for every student with a Synonym A card, there is a a student with a Synonym B card.

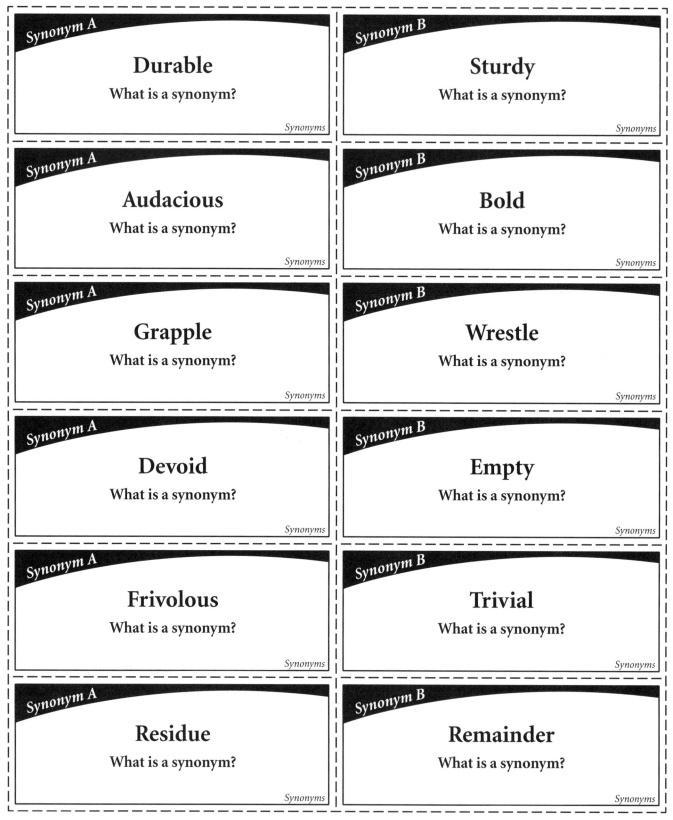

Synonym A

Durable

What is a synonym?

Synonyms

Synonym B

Sturdy

What is a synonym?

Synonyms

Synonym A

Audacious

What is a synonym?

Synonyms

Synonym B

Bold

What is a synonym?

Synonyms

Synonym A

Grapple

What is a synonym?

Synonyms

Synonym B

Wrestle

What is a synonym?

Synonyms

Synonym A

Devoid

What is a synonym?

Synonyms

Synonym B

Empty

What is a synonym?

Synonyms

Synonym A

Frivolous

What is a synonym?

Synonyms

Synonym B

Trivial

What is a synonym?

Synonyms

Synonym A

Residue

What is a synonym?

Synonyms

Synonym B

Remainder

What is a synonym?

Synonyms

Synonyms *(continued)*

Directions: Cut out cards on dotted line. Give one card to each student. Distribute cards in sequence so for every student with a Synonym A card, there is a a student with a Synonym B card.

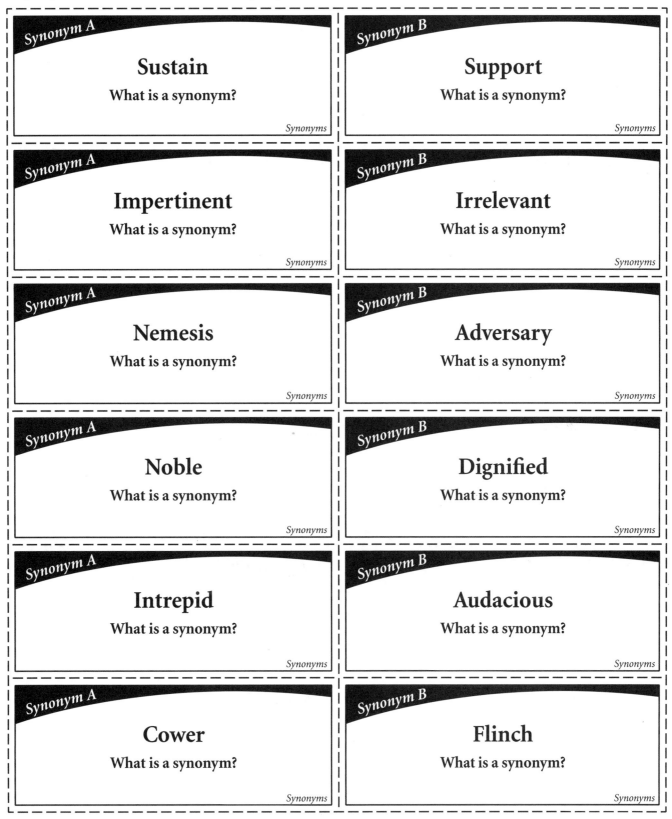

Synonym A	Synonym B
Sustain **What is a synonym?** *Synonyms*	**Support** **What is a synonym?** *Synonyms*
Impertinent **What is a synonym?** *Synonyms*	**Irrelevant** **What is a synonym?** *Synonyms*
Nemesis **What is a synonym?** *Synonyms*	**Adversary** **What is a synonym?** *Synonyms*
Noble **What is a synonym?** *Synonyms*	**Dignified** **What is a synonym?** *Synonyms*
Intrepid **What is a synonym?** *Synonyms*	**Audacious** **What is a synonym?** *Synonyms*
Cower **What is a synonym?** *Synonyms*	**Flinch** **What is a synonym?** *Synonyms*

Synonyms *(continued)*

Directions: Cut out cards on dotted line. Give one card to each student. Distribute cards in sequence so for every student with a Synonym A card, there is a a a student with a Synonym B card.

Synonym A	Synonym B
Sequel What is a synonym? *Synonyms*	**Continuation** What is a synonym? *Synonyms*
Volatile What is a synonym? *Synonyms*	**Erratic** What is a synonym? *Synonyms*
Aghast What is a synonym? *Synonyms*	**Horrified** What is a synonym? *Synonyms*
Cease What is a synonym? *Synonyms*	**Desist** What is a synonym? *Synonyms*
Excise What is a synonym? *Synonyms*	**Delete** What is a synonym? *Synonyms*
Haggard What is a synonym? *Synonyms*	**Gaunt** What is a synonym? *Synonyms*

Synonyms *(continued)*

Directions: Cut out cards on dotted line. Give one card to each student. Distribute cards in sequence so for every student with a Synonym A card, there is a a student with a Synonym B card.

Synonym A	Synonym B
Ravage What is a synonym? *Synonyms*	**Devastate** What is a synonym? *Synonyms*
Wallow What is a synonym? *Synonyms*	**Delight in** What is a synonym? *Synonyms*
Chafe What is a synonym? *Synonyms*	**Irritate** What is a synonym? *Synonyms*
Dire What is a synonym? *Synonyms*	**Disastrous** What is a synonym? *Synonyms*
Disgruntled What is a synonym? *Synonyms*	**Displeased** What is a synonym? *Synonyms*
Encroach What is a synonym? *Synonyms*	**Intrude** What is a synonym? *Synonyms*

Synonyms (continued)

Directions: Cut out cards on dotted line. Give one card to each student. Distribute cards in sequence so for every student with a Synonym A card, there is a a student with a Synonym B card.

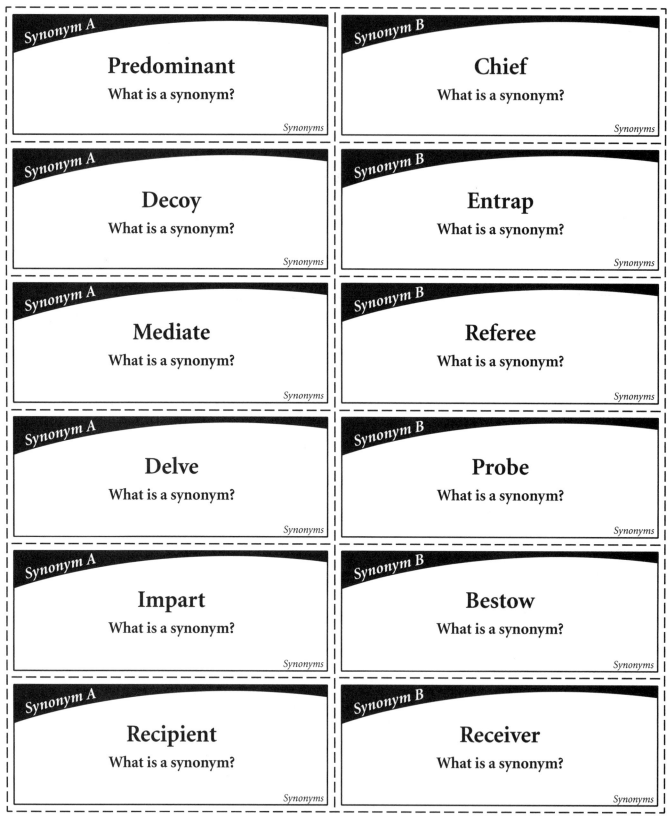

Synonym A

Predominant

What is a synonym?

Synonyms

Synonym B

Chief

What is a synonym?

Synonyms

Synonym A

Decoy

What is a synonym?

Synonyms

Synonym B

Entrap

What is a synonym?

Synonyms

Synonym A

Mediate

What is a synonym?

Synonyms

Synonym B

Referee

What is a synonym?

Synonyms

Synonym A

Delve

What is a synonym?

Synonyms

Synonym B

Probe

What is a synonym?

Synonyms

Synonym A

Impart

What is a synonym?

Synonyms

Synonym B

Bestow

What is a synonym?

Synonyms

Synonym A

Recipient

What is a synonym?

Synonyms

Synonym B

Receiver

What is a synonym?

Synonyms

Figurative Language

Directions: Cut out the cards on the dotted line. Give one card to each student. Distribute cards in sequence so for every student with a Figurative Language card, there is a student with a matching Answer card.

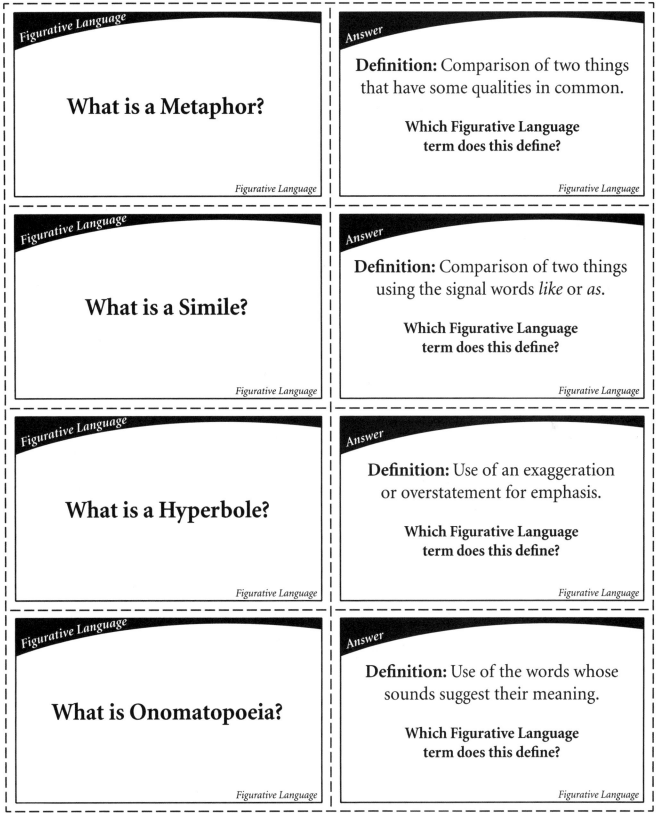

Figurative Language

What is a Metaphor?

Figurative Language

Answer

Definition: Comparison of two things that have some qualities in common.

Which Figurative Language term does this define?

Figurative Language

Figurative Language

What is a Simile?

Figurative Language

Answer

Definition: Comparison of two things using the signal words *like* or *as*.

Which Figurative Language term does this define?

Figurative Language

Figurative Language

What is a Hyperbole?

Figurative Language

Answer

Definition: Use of an exaggeration or overstatement for emphasis.

Which Figurative Language term does this define?

Figurative Language

Figurative Language

What is Onomatopoeia?

Figurative Language

Answer

Definition: Use of the words whose sounds suggest their meaning.

Which Figurative Language term does this define?

Figurative Language

Figurative Language *(continued)*

Directions: Cut out the cards on the dotted line. Give one card to each student. Distribute cards in sequence so for every student with a Figurative Language card, there is a student with a matching Answer card.

Figurative Language

What is Personification?

Figurative Language

Answer

Definition: Giving of human qualities to an animal, object, or an idea.

Which Figurative Language term does this define?

Figurative Language

Figurative Language

What is an Idiom?

Figurative Language

Answer

Definition: Saying that has a special meaning that cannot be understood from the meaning of just the words in the saying.

Which Figurative Language term does this define?

Figurative Language

Figurative Language

What is Analogy?

Figurative Language

Answer

Definition: Point-by-point comparison between two unlike things made to clarify one of the items.

Which Figurative Language term does this define?

Figurative Language

Figurative Language

What is Imagery?

Figurative Language

Answer

Definition: Mental images, which are the product of the imagination.

Which Figurative Language term does this define?

Figurative Language

Figurative Language (continued)

Directions: Cut out the cards on the dotted line. Give one card to each student. Distribute cards in sequence so for every student with a Figurative Language card, there is a student with a matching Answer card.

Figurative Language

What is Assonance?

Figurative Language

Answer

Definition: Repetition of vowel sounds within non-rhyming words.

Which Figurative Language term does this define?

Figurative Language

Figurative Language

What is Alliteration?

Figurative Language

Answer

Definition: Repetition of consonant sounds at the beginning of words.

Which Figurative Language term does this define?

Figurative Language

Figurative Language

What is an Oxymoron?

Figurative Language

Answer

Definition: Phrase with words that contradict each other.

Which Figurative Language term does this define?

Figurative Language

Figurative Language

What is a Paradox?

Figurative Language

Answer

Definition: Statement that seems to contradict itself.

Which Figurative Language term does this define?

Figurative Language

Figurative Language (continued)

Directions: Cut out the cards on the dotted line. Give one card to each student. Distribute cards in sequence so for every student with a Figurative Language card, there is a student with a matching Answer card.

Figurative Language

What is a Pun?

Figurative Language

Answer

Definition: Play on words.

Which Figurative Language term does this define?

Figurative Language

Figurative Language

What is Irony?

Figurative Language

Answer

Definition: Use of words to convey an opposite meaning for their literal meaning.

Which Figurative Language term does this define?

Figurative Language

Figurative Language

What is an Apostrophe?

Figurative Language

Answer

Definition: Breaking off the discourse in a piece of writing in order to address a character, person, or object that is not present.

Which Figurative Language term does this define?

Figurative Language

Figurative Language

Figurative Language

Answer

Figurative Language

Figurative Language
Answer Key

Directions: Use this resource page to introduce students to figurative language and their meanings and/or to check answers.

- **Metaphor**—Comparison of two things that have some qualities in common.

- **Simile**—Comparison of two things using the signal words *like* or *as*.

- **Hyperbole**—Exaggeration or overstatement for emphasis.

- **Onomatopoeia**—Words whose sounds suggest their meaning.

- **Personification**—Giving of human qualities to an animal, object, or an idea.

- **Idiom**—Saying that has a special meaning that cannot be understood from the meaning of just the words in the saying.

- **Analogy**—Point-by-point comparison between two unlike things made to clarify one of the items.

- **Imagery**—Mental images, which are the product of the imagination.

- **Assonance**—Repetition of vowel sounds within non-rhyming words.

- **Alliteration**—Repetition of consonant sounds at the beginning of words.

- **Oxymoron**—Phrase with words that contradict each other.

- **Paradox**—Statement that seems to contradict itself.

- **Pun**—Play on words.

- **Irony**—Use of words to convey an opposite meaning for their literal meaning.

- **Apostrophe**—Breaking off the discourse in a piece of writing in order to address a character, person, or object that is not present.

Parts of Speech

Directions: Cut out cards along the dotted line. Give one card to each student. Distribute cards in sequence so for every student with a Question card, there is a student with a matching Example card.

Question
 	
Theater
This word is a(n):
    Common Noun
    Coordinating conjunction
    Verb
    Adjective
 	
Parts of Speech
	Example
	
	Common Noun
	
	Name an example.
	
	Parts of Speech

Question
 	
Trudy
This word is a(n):
    Adverb
    Common Noun
    Proper Noun
    Interjection
 	
Parts of Speech
	Example
	
	Proper Noun
	
	Name an example.
	
	Parts of Speech

Question
 	
Important
This word is a(n):
    Article
    Adjective
    Linking Verb
    Interjection
 	
Parts of Speech
	Example
	
	Adjective
	
	Name an example.
	
	Parts of Speech

Question
 	
Slowly
This word is a(n):
    Action Verb
    Adverb
    Interjection
    Adjective
 	
Parts of Speech
	Example
	
	Adverb
	
	Name an example.
	
	Parts of Speech

Parts of Speech (continued)

Directions: Cut out cards along the dotted line. Give one card to each student. Distribute cards in sequence so for every student with a Question card, there is a student with a matching Example card.

Question

Under
This word is a:
Proper Noun
Coordinating Conjunction
Preposition
Verb

Parts of Speech

Example

Preposition
Name an example.

Parts of Speech

Question

The
This word is a(n):
Article
Common Noun
Adverb
Action Verb

Parts of Speech

Example

Article
Name an example.

Parts of Speech

Question

Is
This word is a(n):
Preposition
Auxiliary Verb
Linking Verb
Adverb

Parts of Speech

Example

Linking Verb
Name an example.

Parts of Speech

Question

Juan
This word is a:
Common Noun
Interjection
Coordinating Conjunction
Proper Noun

Parts of Speech

Example

Proper Noun
Name an example.

Parts of Speech

Parts of Speech *(continued)*

Directions: Cut out cards along the dotted line. Give one card to each student. Distribute cards in sequence so for every student with a Question card, there is a student with a matching Example card.

Question

Quickly
This word is a(n):
- Prepositional Phrase
- Adjective
- Adverb
- Action Verb

Parts of Speech

Example

Adverb
Name an example.

Parts of Speech

Question

Swished
This word is a(n):
- Article
- Action Verb
- Linking Verb
- Adjective

Parts of Speech

Example

Action Verb
Name an example.

Parts of Speech

Question

Above
This word is a(n):
- Adverb
- Article
- Preposition
- Interjection

Parts of Speech

Example

Preposition
Name an example.

Parts of Speech

Question

And
This word is a(n):
- Coordinating Conjunction
- Linking Verb
- Auxiliary Verb
- Verb

Parts of Speech

Example

Coordinating Conjunction
Name an example.

Parts of Speech

Parts of Speech (continued)

Directions: Cut out cards along the dotted line. Give one card to each student. Distribute cards in sequence so for every student with a Question card, there is a student with a matching Example card.

Question

Hey

This word is a(n):
- Coordinating Conjunction
- Interjection
- Adjective
- Preposition

Parts of Speech

Example

Interjection

Name an example.

Parts of Speech

Question

Walking

This word is a(n):
- Adverb
- Auxiliary Verb
- Action Verb
- Linking Verb

Parts of Speech

Example

Action Verb

Name an example.

Parts of Speech

Question

Within its walls

This word is a(n):
a. Interjection
b. Coordinating Conjunction
c. Prepositional Phrase
d. Auxiliary Verb

Parts of Speech

Example

Prepositional Phrase

Name an example.

Parts of Speech

Question

Me

This word is a(n):
- Article
- Objective Personal Pronoun
- Common Noun
- Proper Noun

Parts of Speech

Example

Objective Personal Pronoun

Name an example.

Parts of Speech

Parts of Speech (continued)

Directions: Cut out cards along the dotted line. Give one card to each student. Distribute cards in sequence so for every student with a Question card, there is a student with a matching Example card.

Question

Everything
This word is a(n):
- Verb
- Adverb
- Interjection
- Indefinite Pronoun

Parts of Speech

Example

Indefinite Pronoun
Name an example.

Parts of Speech

Question

Sways
This word is a(n):
- Adjective
- Linking Verb
- Action Verb
- Auxiliary Verb

Parts of Speech

Example

Verb
Name an example.

Parts of Speech

Question

Be
This word is a(n):
- Auxiliary Verb
- Action Verb
- Linking Verb
- Verb

Parts of Speech

Example

Auxiliary Verb
Name an example.

Parts of Speech

Question

So
This word is a(n):
- Article
- Coordinating Conjunction
- Prepositional Phrase
- Interjection

Parts of Speech

Example

Coordinating Conjunction
Name an example.

Parts of Speech

Parts of Speech *(continued)*

Directions: Cut out cards along the dotted line. Give one card to each student. Distribute cards in sequence so for every student with a Question card, there is a student with a matching Example card.

Question

Oh no
This word is a(n):
  Interjection
  Adjective
  Action Verb
  Coordinating Conjunction

Parts of Speech

Example

Interjection
Name an example.

Parts of Speech

Question

Shall
This word is a(n):
  Action Verb
  Linking Verb
  Verb
  Auxiliary Verb

Parts of Speech

Example

Auxiliary Verb
Name an example.

Parts of Speech

Question

Several
This word is a(n):
  Proper Noun
  Common Noun
  Article
  Indefinite Pronoun

Parts of Speech

Example

Indefinite Pronoun
Name an example.

Parts of Speech

Question

Them
This word is a(n):
  Objective Personal Pronoun
  Preposition
  Common Noun
  Indefinite Pronoun

Parts of Speech

Example

Objective Personal Pronoun
Name an example.

Parts of Speech

Parts of Speech (continued)

Directions: Cut out cards along the dotted line. Give one card to each student. Distribute cards in sequence so for every student with a Question card, there is a student with a matching Example card.

Question	Example
Green This word is a(n): 　Adverb 　Auxiliary Verb 　Article 　Adjective *Parts of Speech*	**Adjective** Name an example. *Parts of Speech*
We This word is a(n): 　Preposition 　Indefinite Pronoun 　Personal Pronoun 　Article *Parts of Speech*	**Personal Pronoun** Name an example. *Parts of Speech*
Toward This word is a(n): 　Preposition 　Linking Verb 　Prepositional Phrase 　Coordinating Conjunction *Parts of Speech*	**Preposition** Name an example. *Parts of Speech*
For various tasks This word is a(n): 　Interjection 　Coordinating Conjunction 　Preposition 　Prepositional Phrase *Parts of Speech*	**Prepositional Phrase** Name an example. *Parts of Speech*

Parts of Speech (continued)

Directions: Cut out cards along the dotted line. Give one card to each student. Distribute cards in sequence so for every student with a Question card, there is a student with a matching Example card.

Question

Wow

This word is a(n):
- Adjective
- Interjection
- Action Verb
- Auxiliary Verb

Parts of Speech

Example

Interjection

Name an example.

Parts of Speech

Question

Yet

This word is a(n):
- Coordinating Conjunction
- Common Noun
- Preposition
- Interjection

Parts of Speech

Example

Coordinating Conjunction

Name an example.

Parts of Speech

Question

Beyond the borders

This word is a(n):
- Coordinating Conjunction
- Adjective
- Prepositional Phrase
- Interjection

Parts of Speech

Example

Prepositional Phrase

Name an example.

Parts of Speech

Question

Toppled

This word is a(n):
- Adverb
- Action Verb
- Auxiliary Verb
- Linking Verb

Parts of Speech

Example

Action Verb

Name an example.

Parts of Speech

Parts of Speech
Answer Key

Directions: Use this resource page to introduce students to parts of speech and their meanings and/or to check answers.

- **Action Verb**—A word that describes an act or activity.
  Examples: Swished, Walking, Toppled

- **Adjective**—A word serving as a modifier of a noun to specify a thing as distinct from something else.
  Examples: Important, Green

- **Adverb**—A word used as a modifier of a verb or adjective, expressing quality, place, time, degree, number, etc.
  Examples: Slowly, Quickly

- **Article**—Any of a small set of words or affixes used with nouns to limit or give finiteness to the application.
  Example: The

- **Auxiliary Verb**—A word used in construction with, and preceding, certain forms of other verbs.
  Examples: Be, Shall

- **Common Noun**—A noun that may be preceded by an article or other limiting modifier and that denotes an entity, not an individual.
  Example: Theater

- **Coordinating Conjunction**—A conjunction that connects two grammatical elements of identical construction.
  Examples: And, So, Yet

- **Indefinite Pronoun**—A pronoun that leaves unspecified the identity of its referent.
  Examples: Everything, Several

- **Interjection**—A word or phrase expressive of emotion; uttering an exclamation.
  Examples: Hey, Oh no, Wow

- **Linking Verb**—A word or expression that links a subject with its predicate.
  Example: Is

- **Objective Personal Pronoun**—The pronoun in a sentence that works as an object of verbs, compound verbs, prepositions, or infinitive phrases.
  Examples: Me, Them

- **Personal Pronoun**—A word that is used to refer to the speaker, or to one or more, or about whom, about which he or she is speaking.
  Example: We

- **Preposition**—A word that is used before nouns, pronouns, or other substantives to form phrases functioning as modifiers of verbs, nouns, or adjectives.
  Examples: Under, Above, Toward

- **Prepositional Phrase**—A phrase consisting of a preposition and its object, usually a noun or a pronoun.
  Examples: Within the walls, For various tasks, Beyond the borders

- **Proper Noun**—A noun that is used to denote a particular person, place, or thing.
  Examples: Trudy, Juan

- **Verb**—A word that expresses an act, occurrence, or mode of being, and has descriptive meaning.
  Example: Sways

Blank Cards Template

Teacher Directions: Use this Blank Cards Template to make your own cards for Mix-N-Match.

Question	Answer
Question	Answer
Question	Answer
Question	Answer
Question	Answer
Question	Answer

Blank Cards Template

Teacher Directions: Use this Blank Cards Template to make your own cards for Mix-N-Match.

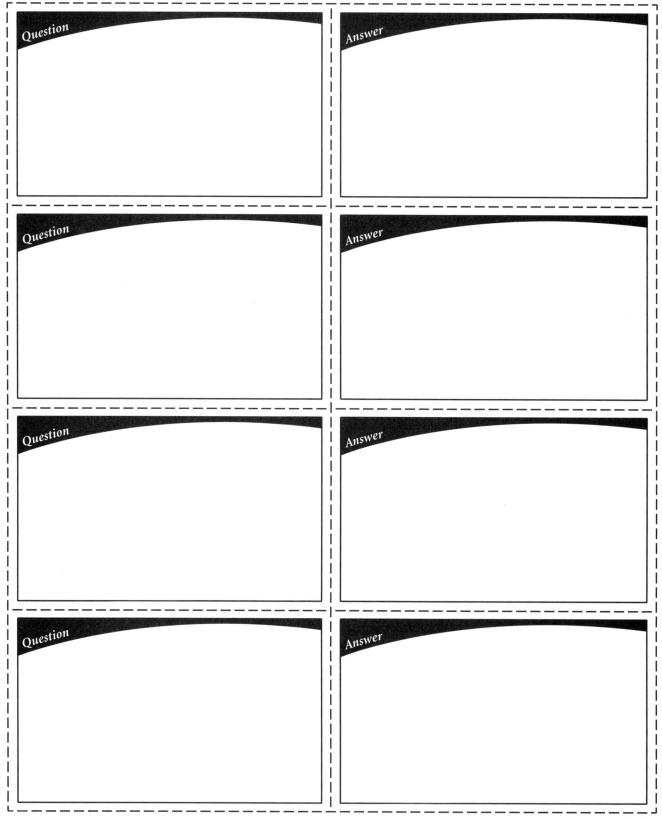

Question

Answer

Question

Answer

Question

Answer

Question

Answer

Showdown
Structure 4

Structure 4
Showdown

When the Showdown Captain calls, "Showdown!" teammates all display their own answers. Teammates either celebrate, or tutor and then celebrate.

Group Size
Teams of Four

Steps

Setup: Teams each have a set of question cards stacked facedown in the center of the table.

1 **Teacher Selects Showdown Captain**
The teacher selects one student on each team to be the Showdown Captain for the first round.

2 **Showdown Captain Reads Question**
The Showdown Captain draws the top card, reads the question, and provides think time.

3 **Students Answer Independently**
Working alone, all students, including the Showdown Captain, write their answers.

4 **Teammates Signal When Done**
When finished, teammates signal they're ready.

5 **Showdown Captain Calls, "Showdown"**
The Showdown Captain calls, "*Showdown.*"

6 **Teams Show Answers**
Teammates show and discuss their answers.

7 **Teams Check for Accuracy**
The Showdown Captain leads the checking.

8 **Celebrate or Coach**
If correct, the team celebrates; if not, teammates tutor, then celebrate.

9 **Rotate Captain Role**
The person on the left of the Showdown Captain becomes the Showdown Captain for the next round.

Modifications: Rather than cards, students can play Showdown with oral questions from the teacher, or from questions on a handout or questions displayed by a projector.

Tips
• Laminate cards for durability for future use.
• Keep team card sets together using a rubber band, paper clip, or envelope.

Activities

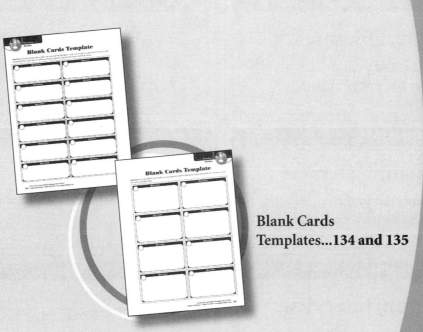

Blank Cards
Templates...134 and 135

The Prefix Is...

Directions: Copy a set of cards for each team. Cut out the cards on the dotted line. Fold cards on solid line and tape or glue the Question and Answer card back to back.

① Question

Premonition, Precede

What is the prefix?
What does the prefix mean?

① Answer

Prefix: pre
Meaning: before

② Question

Postmark, Postpaid

What is the prefix?
What does the prefix mean?

② Answer

Prefix: post
Meaning: after

③ Question

Epilogue, Epicenter

What is the prefix?
What does the prefix mean?

③ Answer

Prefix: epi
Meaning: upon or above

④ Question

Astronaut, Asterik

What is the prefix?
What does the prefix mean?

④ Answer

Prefix: ast
Meaning: star

⑤ Question

Interjection, Interview

What is the prefix?
What does the prefix mean?

⑤ Answer

Prefix: inter
Meaning: between

⑥ Question

Transpose, Transcript

What is the prefix?
What does the prefix mean?

⑥ Answer

Prefix: trans
Meaning: across

The Prefix Is... (continued)

Directions: Copy a set of cards for each team. Cut out the cards on the dotted line. Fold cards on solid line and tape or glue the Question and Answer card back to back.

7 | **Question**

Subject, Subgroup

What is the prefix?
What does the prefix mean?

7 | **Answer**

Prefix: sub
Meaning: under

8 | **Question**

Circumstance, Circumspect

What is the prefix?
What does the prefix mean?

8 | **Answer**

Prefix: circum
Meaning: around

9 | **Question**

Ultramodern, Ultramicroscopic

What is the prefix?
What does the prefix mean?

9 | **Answer**

Prefix: ultra
Meaning: excessive

10 | **Question**

Reimburse, Retell

What is the prefix?
What does the prefix mean?

10 | **Answer**

Prefix: re
Meaning: again

11 | **Question**

Extracurricular, Extramarital

What is the prefix?
What does the prefix mean?

11 | **Answer**

Prefix: extra
Meaning: outside or additional

12 | **Question**

Depart, Defect

What is the prefix?
What does the prefix mean?

12 | **Answer**

Prefix: de
Meaning: away or off

The Prefix Is... *(continued)*

Directions: Copy a set of cards for each team. Cut out the cards on the dotted line. Fold cards on solid line and tape or glue the Question and Answer card back to back.

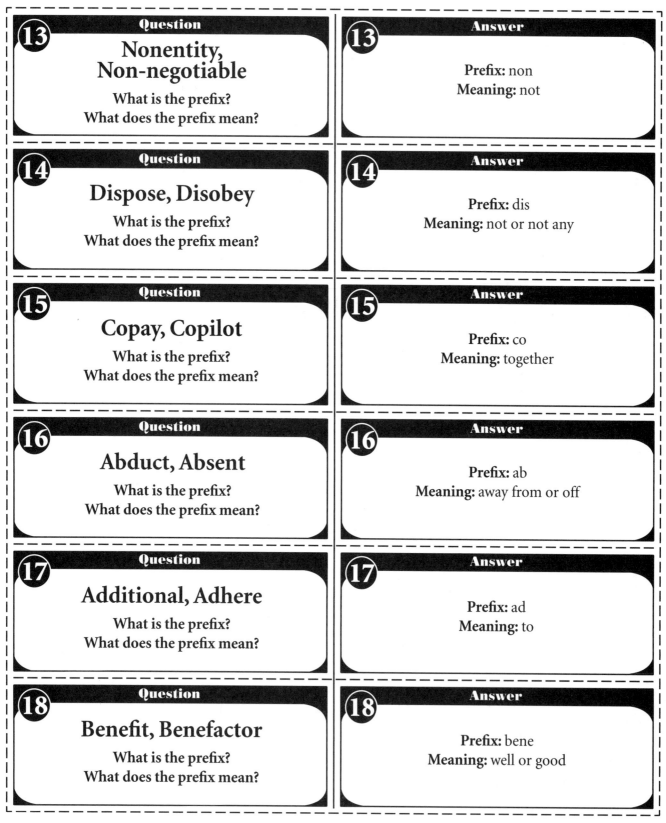

13 | **Question**
Nonentity, Non-negotiable
What is the prefix?
What does the prefix mean?

13 | **Answer**
Prefix: non
Meaning: not

14 | **Question**
Dispose, Disobey
What is the prefix?
What does the prefix mean?

14 | **Answer**
Prefix: dis
Meaning: not or not any

15 | **Question**
Copay, Copilot
What is the prefix?
What does the prefix mean?

15 | **Answer**
Prefix: co
Meaning: together

16 | **Question**
Abduct, Absent
What is the prefix?
What does the prefix mean?

16 | **Answer**
Prefix: ab
Meaning: away from or off

17 | **Question**
Additional, Adhere
What is the prefix?
What does the prefix mean?

17 | **Answer**
Prefix: ad
Meaning: to

18 | **Question**
Benefit, Benefactor
What is the prefix?
What does the prefix mean?

18 | **Answer**
Prefix: bene
Meaning: well or good

The Prefix is... (continued)

Directions: Copy a set of cards for each team. Cut out the cards on the dotted line. Fold cards on solid line and tape or glue the Question and Answer card back to back.

19 Question
Microcosm, Microgram
What is the prefix?
What does the prefix mean?

19 Answer
Prefix: micro
Meaning: small

20 Question
Trilogy, Trinity
What is the prefix?
What does the prefix mean?

20 Answer
Prefix: tri
Meaning: three

21 Question
Unwitting, Unjust
What is the prefix?
What does the prefix mean?

21 Answer
Prefix: un
Meaning: not

22 Question
Semiconscious, Semicircle
What is the prefix?
What does the prefix mean?

22 Answer
Prefix: semi
Meaning: partly

23 Question
Psyche, Psychosis
What is the prefix?
What does the prefix mean?

23 Answer
Prefix: psych
Meaning: mind

24 Question
Mispronounce, Misinform
What is the prefix?
What does the prefix mean?

24 Answer
Prefix: mis
Meaning: bad or wrong

The Prefix Is... *(continued)*

Directions: Copy a set of cards for each team. Cut out the cards on the dotted line. Fold cards on solid line and tape or glue the Question and Answer card back to back.

25 **Question**
Compact, Communicate
What is the prefix?
What does the prefix mean?

25 **Answer**
Prefix: com
Meaning: with or together

26 **Question**
Decimal, Decalogue
What is the prefix?
What does the prefix mean?

26 **Answer**
Prefix: dec
Meaning: ten

27 **Question**
Periphery, Perimeter
What is the prefix?
What does the prefix mean?

27 **Answer**
Prefix: peri
Meaning: all around

28 **Question**
Antibiotic, Anti-aircraft
What is the prefix?
What does the prefix mean?

28 **Answer**
Prefix: anti
Meaning: against

29 **Question**
Automobile, Automatic
What is the prefix?
What does the prefix mean?

29 **Answer**
Prefix: auto
Meaning: self

30 **Question**
Macroscopic, Macrobiotic
What is the prefix?
What does the prefix mean?

30 **Answer**
Prefix: macro
Meaning: large

The Prefix Is... *(continued)*

Directions: Copy a set of cards for each team. Cut out the cards on the dotted line. Fold cards on solid line and tape or glue the Question and Answer card back to back.

31 Question	**31** Answer
Contradict, Contraband What is the prefix? What does the prefix mean?	**Prefix:** contra **Meaning:** against

32 Question	**32** Answer
Symphony, Sympathy What is the prefix? What does the prefix mean?	**Prefix:** sym **Meaning:** with or together

33 Question	**33** Answer

34 Question	**34** Answer

35 Question	**35** Answer

36 Question	**36** Answer

The Prefix Is...
Answer Key

Directions: Use this resource page to introduce students to prefixes and/or to check answers.

The Prefix Is...

Prefix: pre
Meaning: before
Examples: Premonition, Precede

Prefix: post
Meaning: after
Examples: Postmark, Postpaid

Prefix: epi
Meaning: upon or above
Examples: Epilogue, Epicenter

Prefix: ast
Meaning: star
Examples: Astronaut, Asterik

Prefix: inter
Meaning: between
Examples: Interjection, Interview

Prefix: trans
Meaning: across
Examples: Transpose, Transcript

Prefix: sub
Meaning: under
Examples: Subject, Subgroup

Prefix: circum
Meaning: around
Examples: Circumstance, Circumspect

Prefix: ultra
Meaning: excessive
Examples: Ultramodern, Ultramicroscopic

Prefix: re
Meaning: again
Examples: Reimburse, Retell

Prefix: extra
Meaning: outside or additional
Examples: Extracurricular, Extramarital

Prefix: de
Meaning: away or off
Examples: Depart, Defect

Prefix: non
Meaning: not
Examples: Nonentity, Non-negotiable

Prefix: dis
Meaning: not or not any
Examples: Dispose, Disobey

Prefix: co
Meaning: together
Examples: Copay, Copilot

Prefix: ab
Meaning: away from or off
Examples: Abduct, Absent

Prefix: ad
Meaning: to
Examples: Additional, Adhere

Prefix: bene
Meaning: well or good
Examples: Benefit, Benefactor

Prefix: micro
Meaning: small
Examples: Microcosm, Microgram

Prefix: tri
Meaning: three
Examples: Trilogy, Trinity

Prefix: un
Meaning: not
Examples: Unwitting, Unjust

Prefix: semi
Meaning: partly
Examples: Semiconscious, Semicircle

Prefix: psych
Meaning: mind
Examples: Psyche, Psychosis

Prefix: mis
Meaning: bad or wrong
Examples: Mispronounce, Misinform

Prefix: com
Meaning: with or together
Examples: Compact, Communicate

Prefix: dec
Meaning: ten
Examples: Decimal, Decalogue

Prefix: peri
Meaning: all around
Examples: Periphery, Perimeter

Prefix: anti
Meaning: against
Examples: Antibiotic, Anti-aircraft

Prefix: auto
Meaning: self
Examples: Automobile, Automatic

Prefix: macro
Meaning: large
Examples: Macroscopic, Macrobiotic

Prefix Examples

Directions: Copy a set of cards for each team. Cut out the cards on the dotted line. Fold cards on solid line and tape or glue the Question and Answer card back to back.

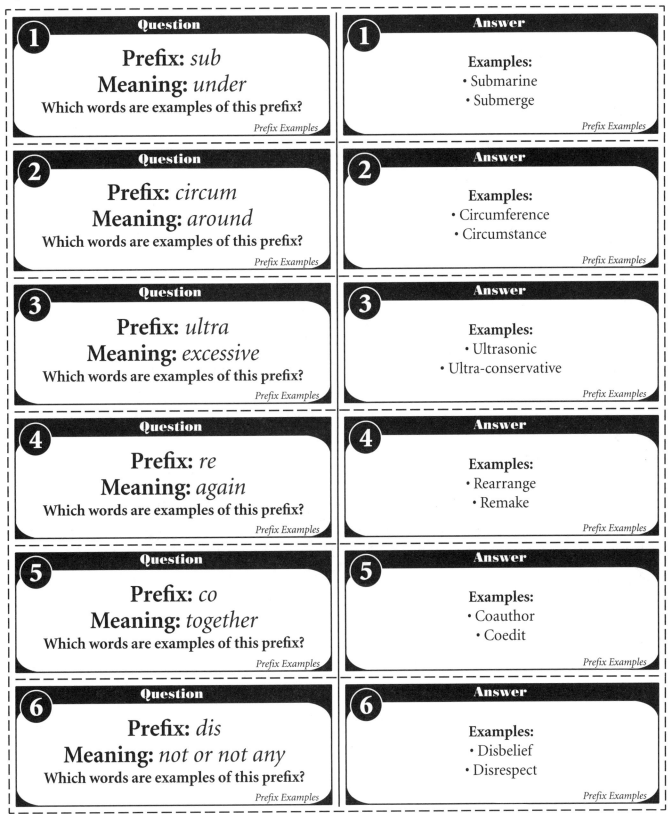

① Question

Prefix: *sub*
Meaning: *under*
Which words are examples of this prefix?
Prefix Examples

① Answer

Examples:
• Submarine
• Submerge
Prefix Examples

② Question

Prefix: *circum*
Meaning: *around*
Which words are examples of this prefix?
Prefix Examples

② Answer

Examples:
• Circumference
• Circumstance
Prefix Examples

③ Question

Prefix: *ultra*
Meaning: *excessive*
Which words are examples of this prefix?
Prefix Examples

③ Answer

Examples:
• Ultrasonic
• Ultra-conservative
Prefix Examples

④ Question

Prefix: *re*
Meaning: *again*
Which words are examples of this prefix?
Prefix Examples

④ Answer

Examples:
• Rearrange
• Remake
Prefix Examples

⑤ Question

Prefix: *co*
Meaning: *together*
Which words are examples of this prefix?
Prefix Examples

⑤ Answer

Examples:
• Coauthor
• Coedit
Prefix Examples

⑥ Question

Prefix: *dis*
Meaning: *not or not any*
Which words are examples of this prefix?
Prefix Examples

⑥ Answer

Examples:
• Disbelief
• Disrespect
Prefix Examples

Prefix Examples *(continued)*

Directions: Copy a set of cards for each team. Cut out the cards on the dotted line. Fold cards on solid line and tape or glue the Question and Answer card back to back.

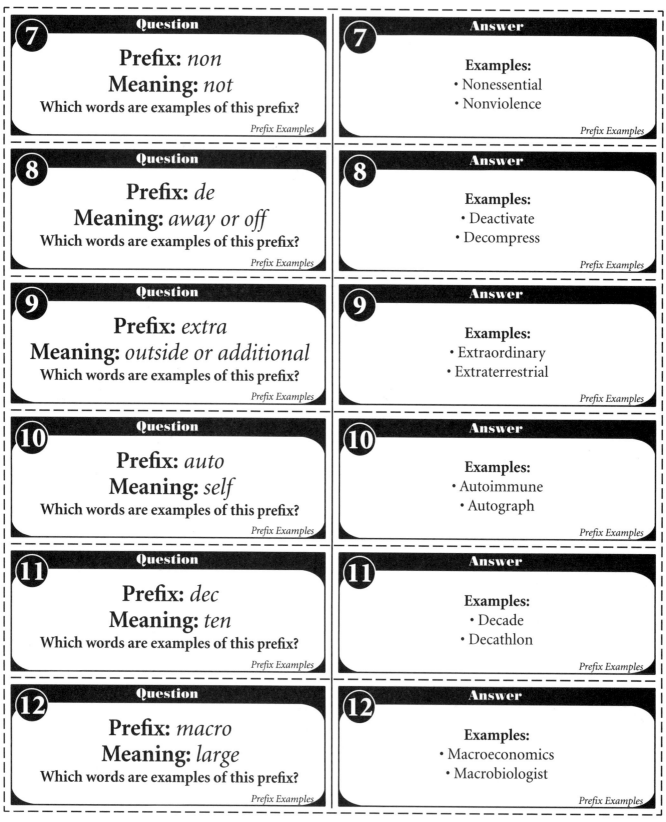

7   **Question**

Prefix: *non*
Meaning: *not*
Which words are examples of this prefix?

Prefix Examples

7   **Answer**

Examples:
• Nonessential
• Nonviolence

Prefix Examples

8   **Question**

Prefix: *de*
Meaning: *away or off*
Which words are examples of this prefix?

Prefix Examples

8   **Answer**

Examples:
• Deactivate
• Decompress

Prefix Examples

9   **Question**

Prefix: *extra*
Meaning: *outside or additional*
Which words are examples of this prefix?

Prefix Examples

9   **Answer**

Examples:
• Extraordinary
• Extraterrestrial

Prefix Examples

10   **Question**

Prefix: *auto*
Meaning: *self*
Which words are examples of this prefix?

Prefix Examples

10   **Answer**

Examples:
• Autoimmune
• Autograph

Prefix Examples

11   **Question**

Prefix: *dec*
Meaning: *ten*
Which words are examples of this prefix?

Prefix Examples

11   **Answer**

Examples:
• Decade
• Decathlon

Prefix Examples

12   **Question**

Prefix: *macro*
Meaning: *large*
Which words are examples of this prefix?

Prefix Examples

12   **Answer**

Examples:
• Macroeconomics
• Macrobiologist

Prefix Examples

Prefix Examples (continued)

Directions: Copy a set of cards for each team. Cut out the cards on the dotted line. Fold cards on solid line and tape or glue the Question and Answer card back to back.

13 **Question**

Prefix: *peri*
Meaning: *all around*
Which words are examples of this prefix?

Prefix Examples

13 **Answer**

Examples:
• Periodontal
• Periscope

Prefix Examples

14 **Question**

Prefix: *anti*
Meaning: *against*
Which words are examples of this prefix?

Prefix Examples

14 **Answer**

Examples:
• Anticlimax
• Antiseptic

Prefix Examples

15 **Question**

Prefix: *mono*
Meaning: *single*
Which words are examples of this prefix?

Prefix Examples

15 **Answer**

Examples:
• Monopoly
• Monotheism

Prefix Examples

16 **Question**

Prefix: *sym*
Meaning: *together*
Which words are examples of this prefix?

Prefix Examples

16 **Answer**

Examples:
• Symmetry
• Symphony

Prefix Examples

17 **Question**

Prefix: *micro*
Meaning: *small*
Which words are examples of this prefix?

Prefix Examples

17 **Answer**

Examples:
• Microscope
• Microchip

Prefix Examples

18 **Question**

Prefix: *cap*
Meaning: *do*
Which words are examples of this prefix?

Prefix Examples

18 **Answer**

Examples:
• Captain
• Capital

Prefix Examples

Prefix Examples (continued)

Directions: Copy a set of cards for each team. Cut out the cards on the dotted line. Fold cards on solid line and tape or glue the Question and Answer card back to back.

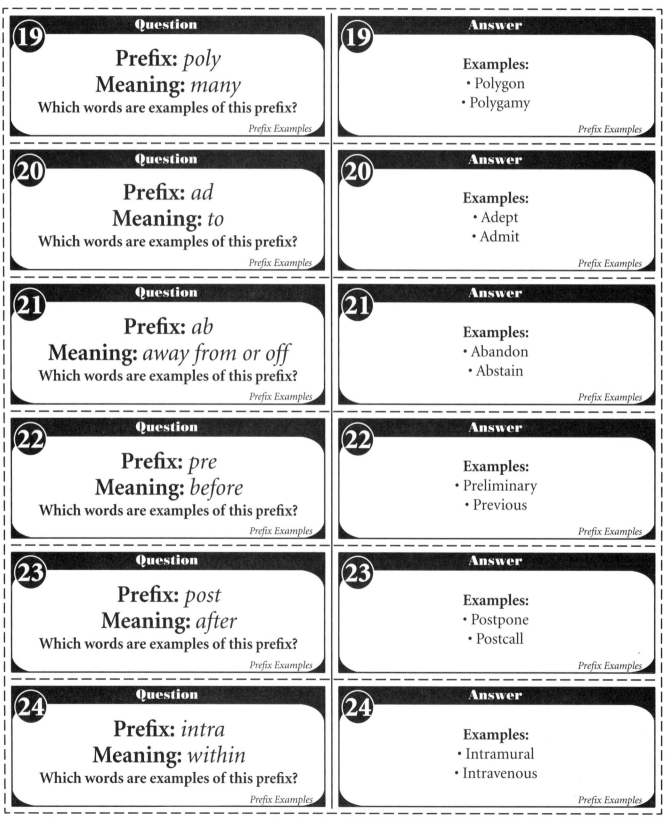

19 | **Question**

Prefix: *poly*
Meaning: *many*
Which words are examples of this prefix?

Prefix Examples

19 | **Answer**

Examples:
- Polygon
- Polygamy

Prefix Examples

20 | **Question**

Prefix: *ad*
Meaning: *to*
Which words are examples of this prefix?

Prefix Examples

20 | **Answer**

Examples:
- Adept
- Admit

Prefix Examples

21 | **Question**

Prefix: *ab*
Meaning: *away from or off*
Which words are examples of this prefix?

Prefix Examples

21 | **Answer**

Examples:
- Abandon
- Abstain

Prefix Examples

22 | **Question**

Prefix: *pre*
Meaning: *before*
Which words are examples of this prefix?

Prefix Examples

22 | **Answer**

Examples:
- Preliminary
- Previous

Prefix Examples

23 | **Question**

Prefix: *post*
Meaning: *after*
Which words are examples of this prefix?

Prefix Examples

23 | **Answer**

Examples:
- Postpone
- Postcall

Prefix Examples

24 | **Question**

Prefix: *intra*
Meaning: *within*
Which words are examples of this prefix?

Prefix Examples

24 | **Answer**

Examples:
- Intramural
- Intravenous

Prefix Examples

Prefix Examples *(continued)*

Directions: Copy a set of cards for each team. Cut out the cards on the dotted line. Fold cards on solid line and tape or glue the Question and Answer card back to back.

25 | Question
Prefix: *ante*
Meaning: *before*
Which words are examples of this prefix?
Prefix Examples

25 | Answer
Examples:
• Antecedent
• Antebellum
Prefix Examples

26 | Question
Prefix: *inter*
Meaning: *between*
Which words are examples of this prefix?
Prefix Examples

26 | Answer
Examples:
• Interstate
• Interfere
Prefix Examples

27 | Question
Prefix: *trans*
Meaning: *across*
Which words are examples of this prefix?
Prefix Examples

27 | Answer
Examples:
• Transport
• Transaction
Prefix Examples

28 | Question
Prefix: *mis*
Meaning: *bad or wrong*
Which words are examples of this prefix?
Prefix Examples

28 | Answer
Examples:
• Misconception
• Mistake
Prefix Examples

29 | Question
Prefix: *un*
Meaning: *not*
Which words are examples of this prefix?
Prefix Examples

29 | Answer
Examples:
• Unfounded
• Unable
Prefix Examples

30 | Question
Prefix: *bene*
Meaning: *well or good*
Which words are examples of this prefix?
Prefix Examples

30 | Answer
Examples:
• Benefactor
• Benign
Prefix Examples

Prefix Examples (continued)

Directions: Copy a set of cards for each team. Cut out the cards on the dotted line. Fold cards on solid line and tape or glue the Question and Answer card back to back.

31 Question

Prefix: *dia*
Meaning: *through or across*
Which words are examples of this prefix?

Prefix Examples

31 Answer

Examples:
• Diameter
• Diametric

Prefix Examples

32 Question

Prefix: *hemi*
Meaning: *half*
Which words are examples of this prefix?

Prefix Examples

32 Answer

Examples:
• Hemisphere
• Hemicylindrical

Prefix Examples

33 Question

Prefix Examples

33 Answer

Prefix Examples

34 Question

Prefix Examples

34 Answer

Prefix Examples

35 Question

Prefix Examples

35 Answer

Prefix Examples

36 Question

Prefix Examples

36 Answer

Prefix Examples

Text Structure Signal Words

Directions: Copy a set of cards for each team. Cut out the cards on the dotted line. Students select the correct Text Structure Signal Words Answer Cards to answer each question.

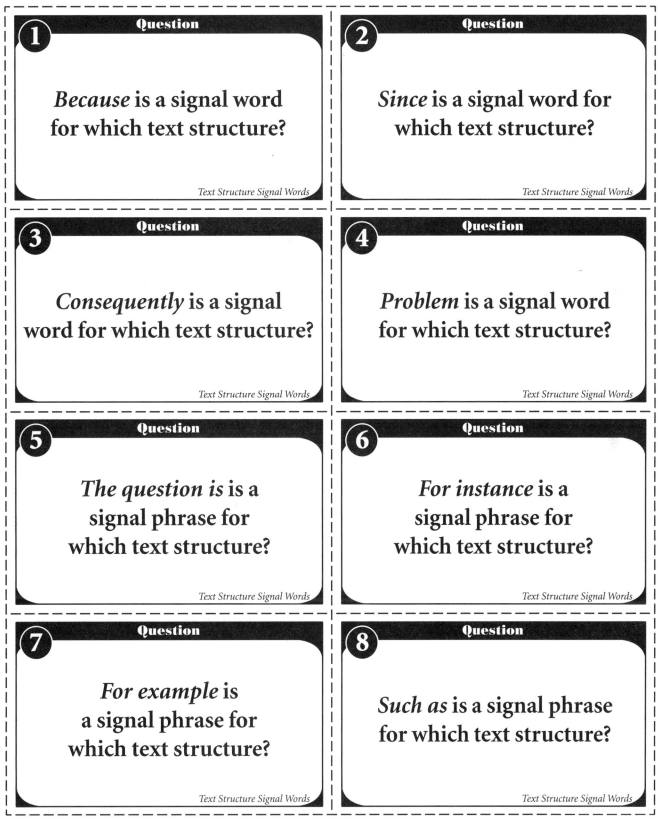

① Question

Because is a signal word for which text structure?

Text Structure Signal Words

② Question

Since is a signal word for which text structure?

Text Structure Signal Words

③ Question

Consequently is a signal word for which text structure?

Text Structure Signal Words

④ Question

Problem is a signal word for which text structure?

Text Structure Signal Words

⑤ Question

The question is is a signal phrase for which text structure?

Text Structure Signal Words

⑥ Question

For instance is a signal phrase for which text structure?

Text Structure Signal Words

⑦ Question

For example is a signal phrase for which text structure?

Text Structure Signal Words

⑧ Question

Such as is a signal phrase for which text structure?

Text Structure Signal Words

Text Structure Signal Words (continued)

Directions: Copy a set of cards for each team. Cut out the cards on the dotted line. Students select the correct Text Structure Signal Words Answer Cards to answer each question.

9 | **Question**

Same as is a signal phrase for which text structure?

Text Structure Signal Words

10 | **Question**

Different from is a signal phrase for which text structure?

Text Structure Signal Words

11 | **Question**

Similar to is a signal phrase for which text structure?

Text Structure Signal Words

12 | **Question**

Last of all is a signal phrase for which text structure?

Text Structure Signal Words

13 | **Question**

Second is a signal word for which text structure?

Text Structure Signal Words

14 | **Question**

Next is a signal word for which text structure?

Text Structure Signal Words

15 | **Question**

Then is a signal word for which text structure?

Text Structure Signal Words

16 | **Question**

This led to is a signal phrase for which text structure?

Text Structure Signal Words

Text Structure Signal Words *(continued)*

Directions: Copy a set of cards for each team. Cut out the cards on the dotted line. Students select the correct Text Structure Signal Words Answer Cards to answer each question.

17 | Question

So that is a signal phrase for which text structure?

Text Structure Signal Words

18 | Question

Nevertheless is a signal word for which text structure?

Text Structure Signal Words

19 | Question

A solution is a signal phrase for which text structure?

Text Structure Signal Words

20 | Question

One answer is a signal phrase for which text structure?

Text Structure Signal Words

21 | Question

One reason for the problem is a signal phrase for which text structure?

Text Structure Signal Words

22 | Question

To illustrate is a signal phrase for which text structure?

Text Structure Signal Words

23 | Question

Most important is a signal phrase for which text structure?

Text Structure Signal Words

24 | Question

In addition is a signal phrase for which text structure?

Text Structure Signal Words

Text Structure Signal Words _(continued)

Directions: Copy a set of cards for each team. Cut out the cards on the dotted line. Students select the correct Text Structure Signal Words Answer Cards to answer each question.

25 Question

Another is a signal word for which text structure?

Text Structure Signal Words

26 Question

Furthermore is a signal word for which text structure?

Text Structure Signal Words

27 Question

Initially is a signal word for which text structure?

Text Structure Signal Words

28 Question

Before is a signal word for which text structure?

Text Structure Signal Words

29 Question

After is a signal word for which text structure?

Text Structure Signal Words

30 Question

When is a signal word for which text structure?

Text Structure Signal Words

31 Question

Finally is a signal word for which text structure?

Text Structure Signal Words

32 Question

Accordingly is a signal word for which text structure?

Text Structure Signal Words

Text Structure Signal Words (continued)

Directions: Copy a set of cards for each team. Cut out the cards on the dotted line. Students select the correct Text Structure Signal Words Answer Cards to answer each question.

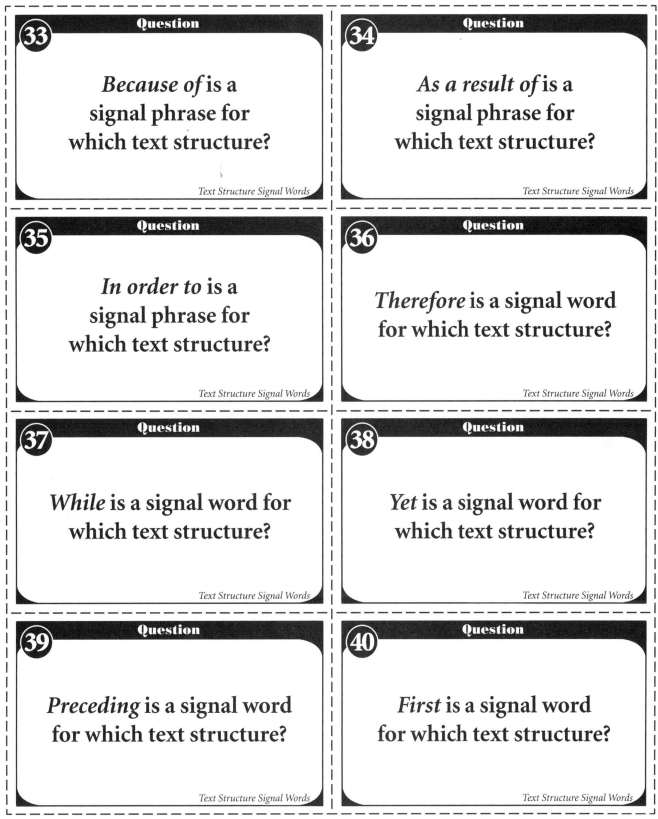

33 Question

Because of is a signal phrase for which text structure?

Text Structure Signal Words

34 Question

As a result of is a signal phrase for which text structure?

Text Structure Signal Words

35 Question

In order to is a signal phrase for which text structure?

Text Structure Signal Words

36 Question

Therefore is a signal word for which text structure?

Text Structure Signal Words

37 Question

While is a signal word for which text structure?

Text Structure Signal Words

38 Question

Yet is a signal word for which text structure?

Text Structure Signal Words

39 Question

Preceding is a signal word for which text structure?

Text Structure Signal Words

40 Question

First is a signal word for which text structure?

Text Structure Signal Words

Text Structure Signal Words (continued)

Directions: Copy a set of cards for each team. Cut out the cards on the dotted line. Students select the correct Text Structure Signal Words Answer Cards to answer each question.

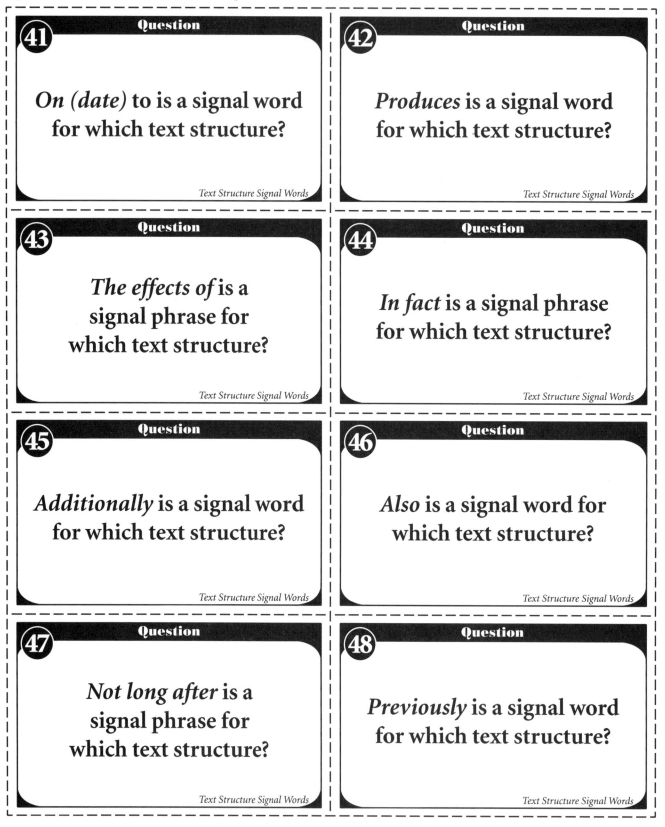

Question

41

On (date) to is a signal word for which text structure?

Text Structure Signal Words

Question

42

Produces is a signal word for which text structure?

Text Structure Signal Words

Question

43

The effects of is a signal phrase for which text structure?

Text Structure Signal Words

Question

44

In fact is a signal phrase for which text structure?

Text Structure Signal Words

Question

45

Additionally is a signal word for which text structure?

Text Structure Signal Words

Question

46

Also is a signal word for which text structure?

Text Structure Signal Words

Question

47

Not long after is a signal phrase for which text structure?

Text Structure Signal Words

Question

48

Previously is a signal word for which text structure?

Text Structure Signal Words

Text Structure Signal Words *(continued)*

Directions: Copy a set of cards for each team. Cut out the cards on the dotted line. Students select the correct Text Structure Signal Words Answer Cards to answer each question.

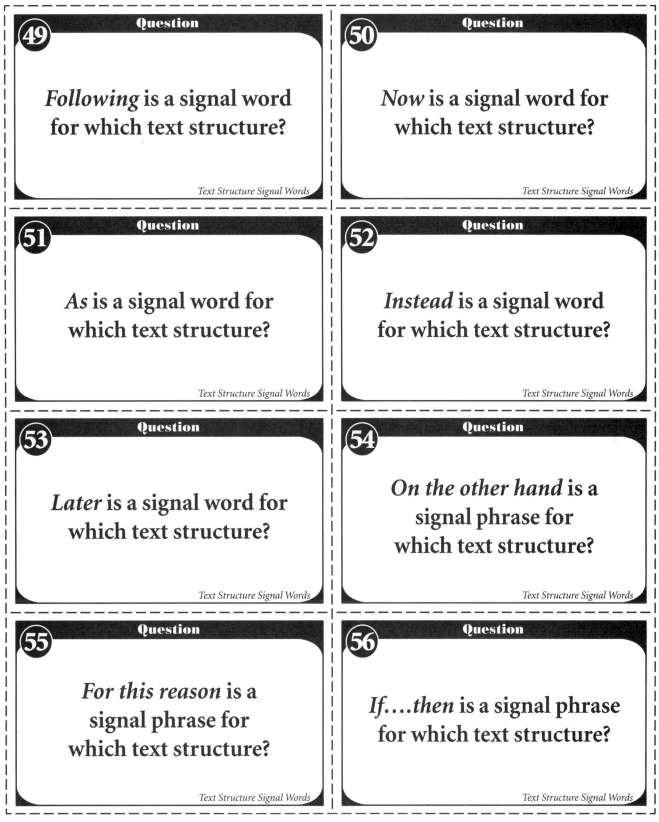

49 Question

Following is a signal word for which text structure?

Text Structure Signal Words

50 Question

Now is a signal word for which text structure?

Text Structure Signal Words

51 Question

As is a signal word for which text structure?

Text Structure Signal Words

52 Question

Instead is a signal word for which text structure?

Text Structure Signal Words

53 Question

Later is a signal word for which text structure?

Text Structure Signal Words

54 Question

On the other hand is a signal phrase for which text structure?

Text Structure Signal Words

55 Question

For this reason is a signal phrase for which text structure?

Text Structure Signal Words

56 Question

If....then is a signal phrase for which text structure?

Text Structure Signal Words

Text Structure Signal Words (continued)

Directions: Copy a set of cards for each team. Cut out the cards on the dotted line. Students select the correct Text Structure Signal Words Answer Cards to answer each question.

Question 57 — *Compared with* is a signal phrase for which text structure? *Text Structure Signal Words*	**Question 58** — *Either…or* is a signal phrase for which text structure? *Text Structure Signal Words*
Question 59 — *But* is a signal word for which text structure? *Text Structure Signal Words*	**Question 60** — *To begin with* is a signal phrase for which text structure? *Text Structure Signal Words*
Question 61 — *Text Structure Signal Words*	**Question 62** — *Text Structure Signal Words*
Question 63 — *Text Structure Signal Words*	**Question 64** — *Text Structure Signal Words*

Text Structure Signal Words
Answer Cards

Directions: Copy enough cards so each student receives a set. Cut out the cards on the dotted line. Students select and show the Text Structure Signal Words Answer Card that corresponds to the Text Structure Signal Words questions.

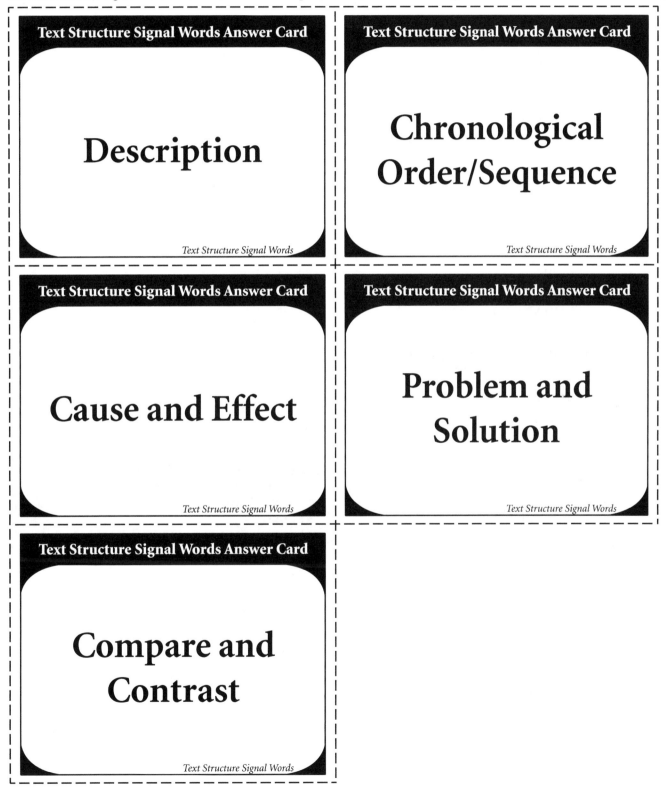

Text Structure Signal Words Answer Card

Description

Text Structure Signal Words

Text Structure Signal Words Answer Card

Chronological Order/Sequence

Text Structure Signal Words

Text Structure Signal Words Answer Card

Cause and Effect

Text Structure Signal Words

Text Structure Signal Words Answer Card

Problem and Solution

Text Structure Signal Words

Text Structure Signal Words Answer Card

Compare and Contrast

Text Structure Signal Words

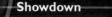

Text Structure Signal Words
Answer Key

Directions: Use this resource page to introduce students to text structure signal words and/or to check answers.

Signal Words

Cause and Effect

- Because
- Since
- Consequently
- This led to
- So that
- Nevertheless
- Accordingly
- Because of
- As a result of
- In order to
- Therefore
- Produces
- The effects of
- For this reason
- If....then

Problem and Solution

- Problem
- The question is
- A solution
- One answer
- One reason for the problem
- As a result of

Description

- For instance
- For example
- Such as
- To illustrate
- Most important
- In addition
- Another
- Furthermore
- To begin with
- Also
- In fact

Chronological Order/Sequence

- First
- Second
- Next
- Then
- Initially
- Before
- After
- When
- Finally
- Additionally
- On (date)
- Preceding
- Not long after
- Previously
- Later
- Following
- Now
- As
- Last of all
- While
- To begin with

Compare and Contrast

- Different from
- Same as
- Similar to
- While
- Yet
- Instead
- On the other hand
- Compared with
- Either...or
- But

Text Structures and Types

Directions: Copy a set of cards for each team. Cut out the cards on the dotted line. Students select the correct Text Structure or Text Type Answer Cards to answer each question.

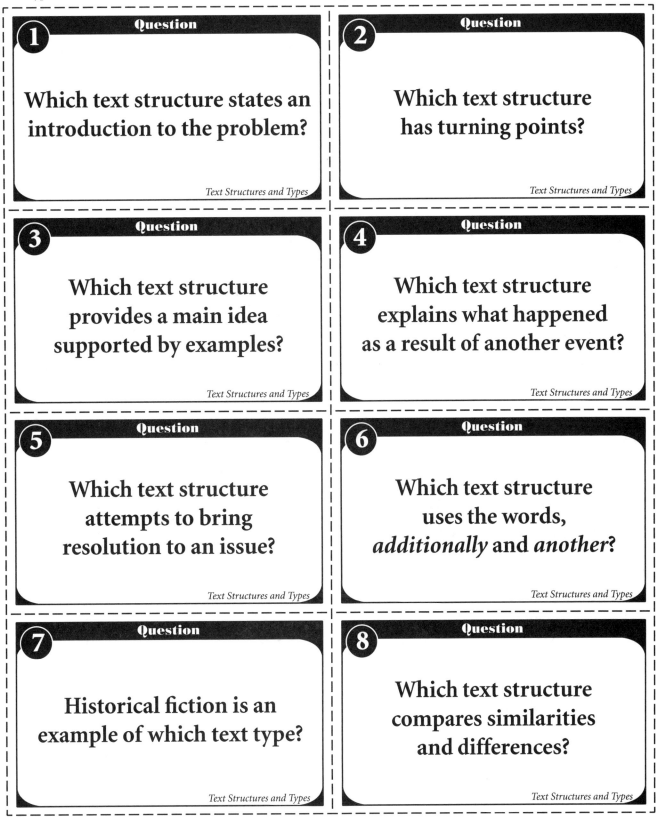

① Question

Which text structure states an introduction to the problem?

Text Structures and Types

② Question

Which text structure has turning points?

Text Structures and Types

③ Question

Which text structure provides a main idea supported by examples?

Text Structures and Types

④ Question

Which text structure explains what happened as a result of another event?

Text Structures and Types

⑤ Question

Which text structure attempts to bring resolution to an issue?

Text Structures and Types

⑥ Question

Which text structure uses the words, *additionally* and *another*?

Text Structures and Types

⑦ Question

Historical fiction is an example of which text type?

Text Structures and Types

⑧ Question

Which text structure compares similarities and differences?

Text Structures and Types

Text Structures and Types *(continued)*

Directions: Copy a set of cards for each team. Cut out the cards on the dotted line. Students select the correct Text Structure or Text Type Answer Cards to answer each question.

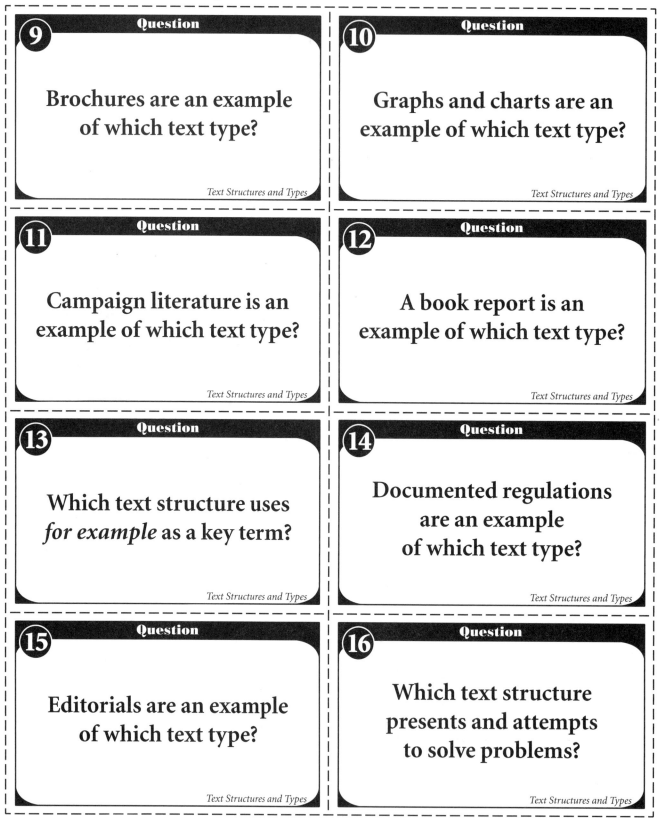

9 Question

Brochures are an example of which text type?

Text Structures and Types

10 Question

Graphs and charts are an example of which text type?

Text Structures and Types

11 Question

Campaign literature is an example of which text type?

Text Structures and Types

12 Question

A book report is an example of which text type?

Text Structures and Types

13 Question

Which text structure uses *for example* as a key term?

Text Structures and Types

14 Question

Documented regulations are an example of which text type?

Text Structures and Types

15 Question

Editorials are an example of which text type?

Text Structures and Types

16 Question

Which text structure presents and attempts to solve problems?

Text Structures and Types

Text Structures and Types (continued)

Directions: Copy a set of cards for each team. Cut out the cards on the dotted line. Students select the correct Text Structure or Text Type Answer Cards to answer each question.

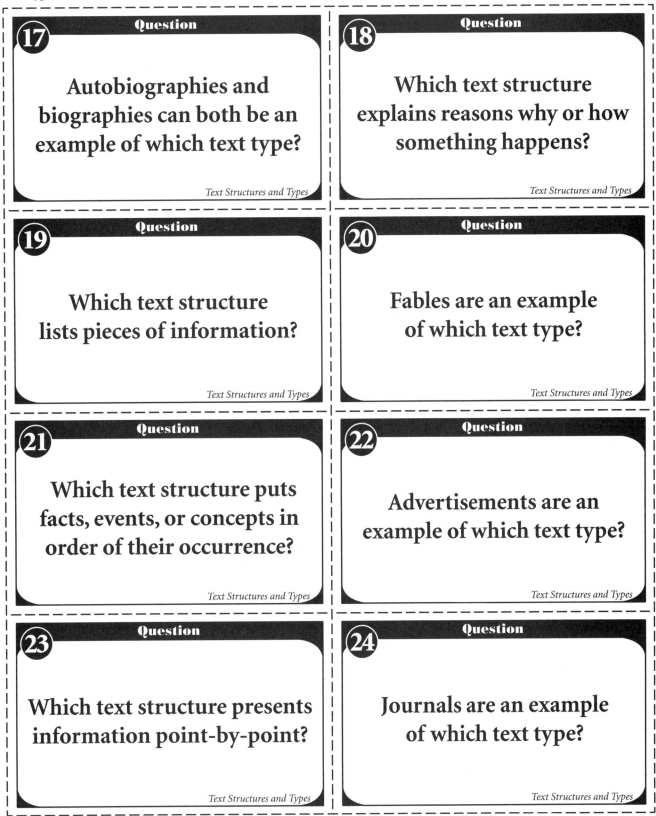

Question 17

Autobiographies and biographies can both be an example of which text type?

Text Structures and Types

Question 18

Which text structure explains reasons why or how something happens?

Text Structures and Types

Question 19

Which text structure lists pieces of information?

Text Structures and Types

Question 20

Fables are an example of which text type?

Text Structures and Types

Question 21

Which text structure puts facts, events, or concepts in order of their occurrence?

Text Structures and Types

Question 22

Advertisements are an example of which text type?

Text Structures and Types

Question 23

Which text structure presents information point-by-point?

Text Structures and Types

Question 24

Journals are an example of which text type?

Text Structures and Types

Text Structures and Types (continued)

Directions: Copy a set of cards for each team. Cut out the cards on the dotted line. Students select the correct Text Structure or Text Type Answer Cards to answer each question.

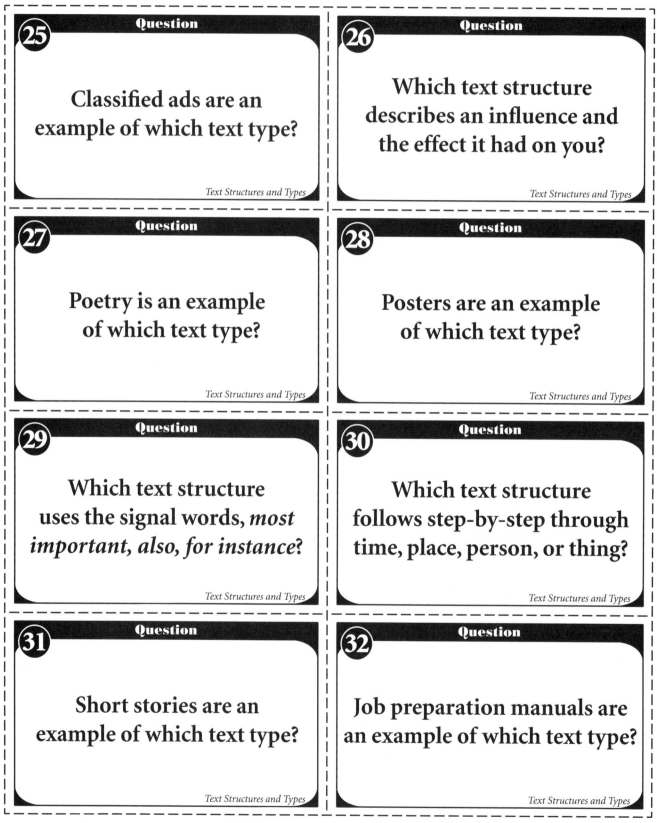

25 Question

Classified ads are an example of which text type?

Text Structures and Types

26 Question

Which text structure describes an influence and the effect it had on you?

Text Structures and Types

27 Question

Poetry is an example of which text type?

Text Structures and Types

28 Question

Posters are an example of which text type?

Text Structures and Types

29 Question

Which text structure uses the signal words, *most important, also, for instance*?

Text Structures and Types

30 Question

Which text structure follows step-by-step through time, place, person, or thing?

Text Structures and Types

31 Question

Short stories are an example of which text type?

Text Structures and Types

32 Question

Job preparation manuals are an example of which text type?

Text Structures and Types

Text Structures and Types (continued)

Directions: Copy a set of cards for each team. Cut out the cards on the dotted line. Students select the correct Text Structure or Text Type Answer Cards to answer each question.

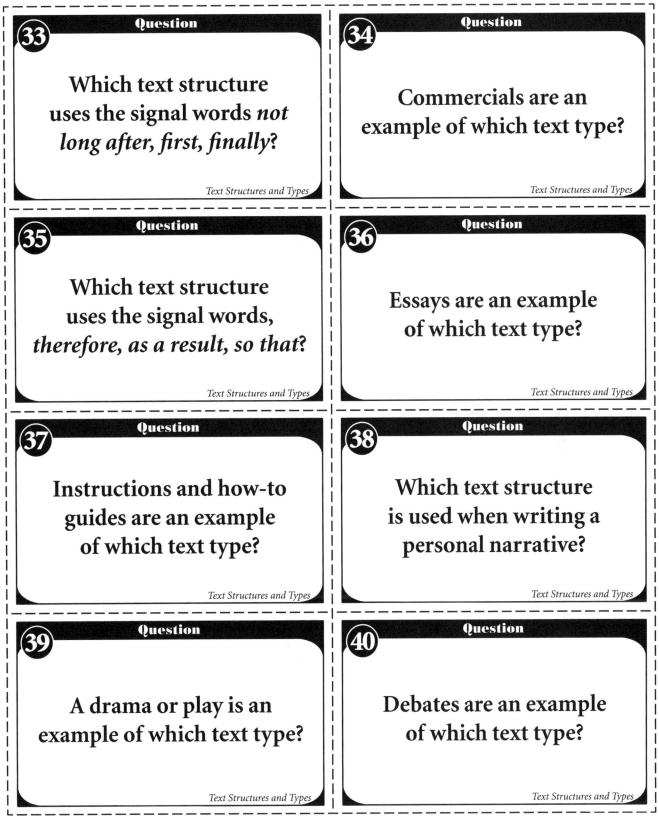

Question 33

Which text structure uses the signal words *not long after, first, finally?*

Text Structures and Types

Question 34

Commercials are an example of which text type?

Text Structures and Types

Question 35

Which text structure uses the signal words, *therefore, as a result, so that?*

Text Structures and Types

Question 36

Essays are an example of which text type?

Text Structures and Types

Question 37

Instructions and how-to guides are an example of which text type?

Text Structures and Types

Question 38

Which text structure is used when writing a personal narrative?

Text Structures and Types

Question 39

A drama or play is an example of which text type?

Text Structures and Types

Question 40

Debates are an example of which text type?

Text Structures and Types

Text Structures and Types *(continued)*

Directions: Copy a set of cards for each team. Cut out the cards on the dotted line. Students select the correct Text Structure or Text Type Answer Cards to answer each question.

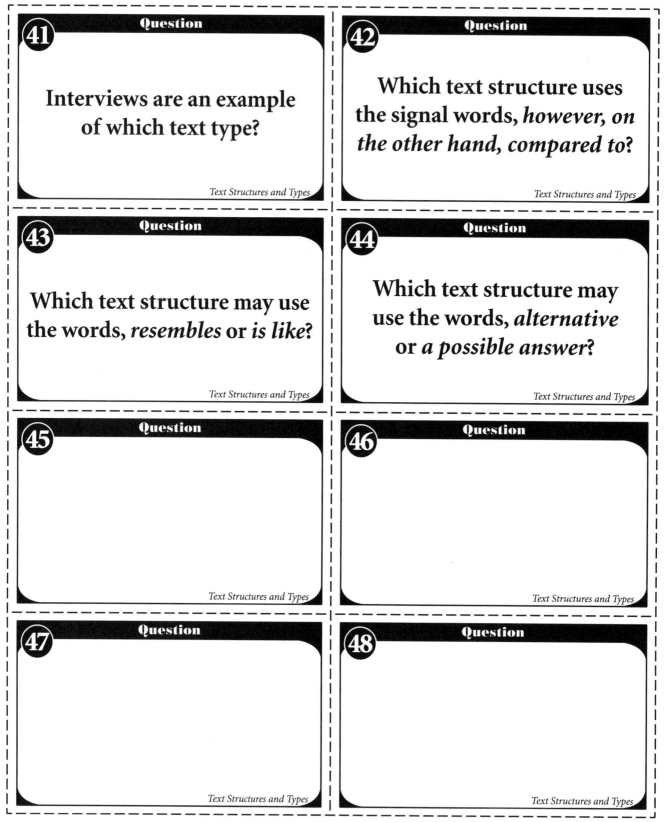

41 **Question**

Interviews are an example of which text type?

Text Structures and Types

42 **Question**

Which text structure uses the signal words, *however, on the other hand, compared to*?

Text Structures and Types

43 **Question**

Which text structure may use the words, *resembles* or *is like*?

Text Structures and Types

44 **Question**

Which text structure may use the words, *alternative* or *a possible answer*?

Text Structures and Types

45 **Question**

Text Structures and Types

46 **Question**

Text Structures and Types

47 **Question**

Text Structures and Types

48 **Question**

Text Structures and Types

Text Structure
Answer Cards

Directions: Copy enough cards so each student receives a set. Cut out the cards on the dotted line. Students select and show the answer card that corresponds to the Text Structures and Types questions.

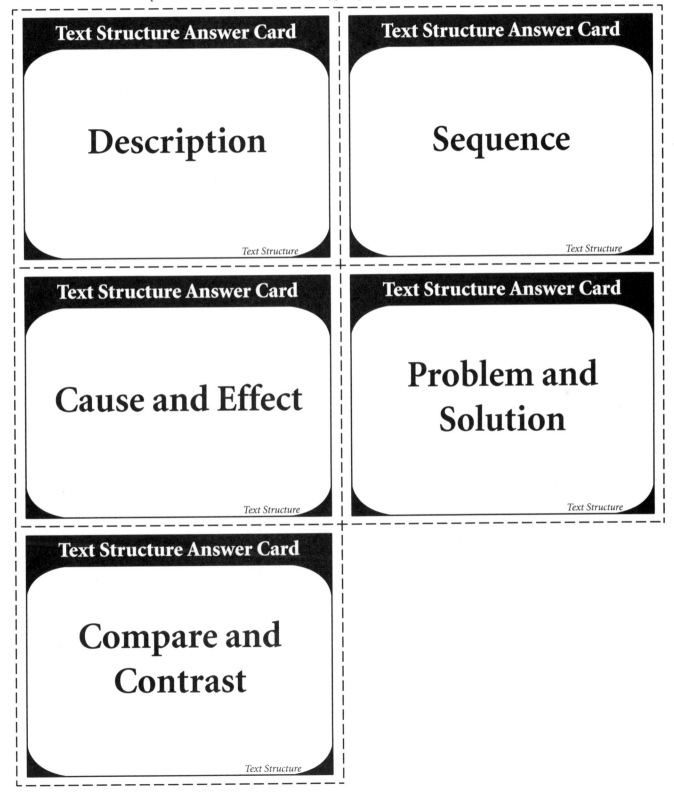

Text Structure Answer Card

Description

Text Structure

Text Structure Answer Card

Sequence

Text Structure

Text Structure Answer Card

Cause and Effect

Text Structure

Text Structure Answer Card

Problem and Solution

Text Structure

Text Structure Answer Card

Compare and Contrast

Text Structure

Text Type
Answer Cards

Directions: Copy enough cards so each student receives a set. Cut out the cards on the dotted line. Students select and show the answer card that corresponds to the Text Structures and Types questions.

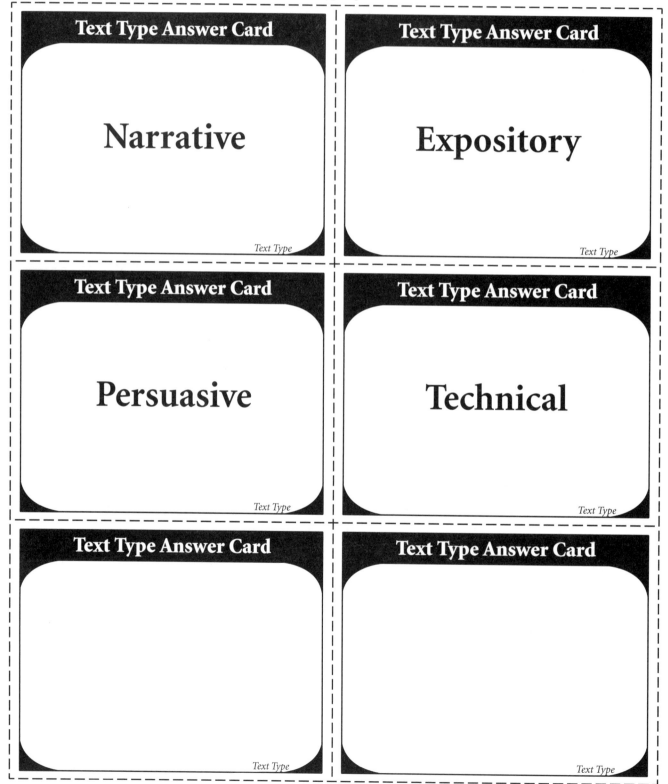

Text Type Answer Card

Narrative

Text Type

Text Type Answer Card

Expository

Text Type

Text Type Answer Card

Persuasive

Text Type

Text Type Answer Card

Technical

Text Type

Text Type Answer Card

Text Type

Text Type Answer Card

Text Type

Text Structures and Types
Answer Key

Directions: Use this resource page to introduce students to text structures and types and/or to check answers.

Text Structures and Types

Narrative Text
Text Type Examples:
- Historical fiction
- Fable
- Poetry
- Short story
- Drama or play

Expository
Text Type Examples:
- Book report
- Autobiography and biography
- Journal
- Essay
- Interview

Persuasive
Text Type Examples:
- Brochure
- Campaign literature
- Editorial
- Advertisement
- Poster
- Commercial
- Debate

Technical
Text Type Examples:
- Graph or chart
- Documented regulation
- Classified ad
- Job preparation manual
- Instructions or how-to guide

Description
Text Structure Examples:
- Uses the words, *additionally* and *another*
- Uses *for example* as a key term
- Provides a main idea supported by examples

- Describes an influence and the effect it had on you
- Uses the signal words, *most important, also, for instance*
- Lists pieces of information

Sequence
Text Structure Examples:
- Includes personal narrative
- Has turning points
- Puts, facts, events, or concepts in order of their occurrence
- Follows step-by-step through time, place, person, or thing
- Uses the signal words *not long after, first, finally*

Compare and Contrast
Text Structure Examples:
- Compares similarities and differences
- Presents information point-by-point
- Uses the signal words *however, on the other hand, compared to*
- May use the words *resembles* or *is like*
- May use the words *alternative* or a *possible answer*

Cause and Effect
Text Structure Examples:
- Explains what happened as a result of another event
- Explains reasons why or how something happens
- Uses the signal words, *therefore, as a result, so that*

Problem and Solution
Text Structure Examples:
- States an introduction to the problem
- Attempts to bring resolution to an issue
- Presents and attempts to solve problems

Blank Cards Template

Directions: Use these blank cards to make your own cards for Showdown. Copy a set of cards for each team. Cut out the cards on the dotted line. Fold cards on solid line and tape or glue the Question and Answer card back to back.

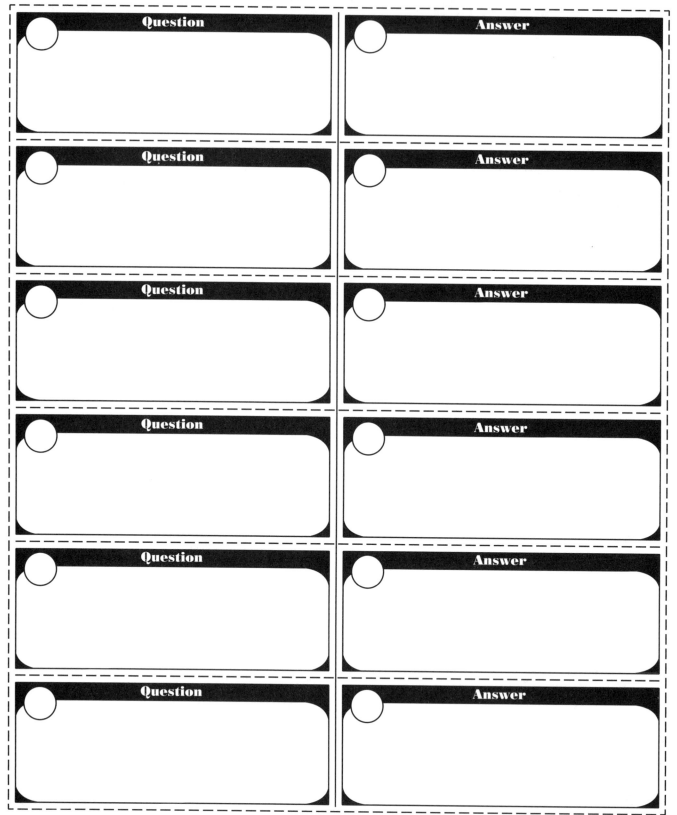

Blank Cards Template

Directions: Use these blank cards to make your own cards for Showdown. Copy a set of cards for each team. Cut out the cards on the dotted line.

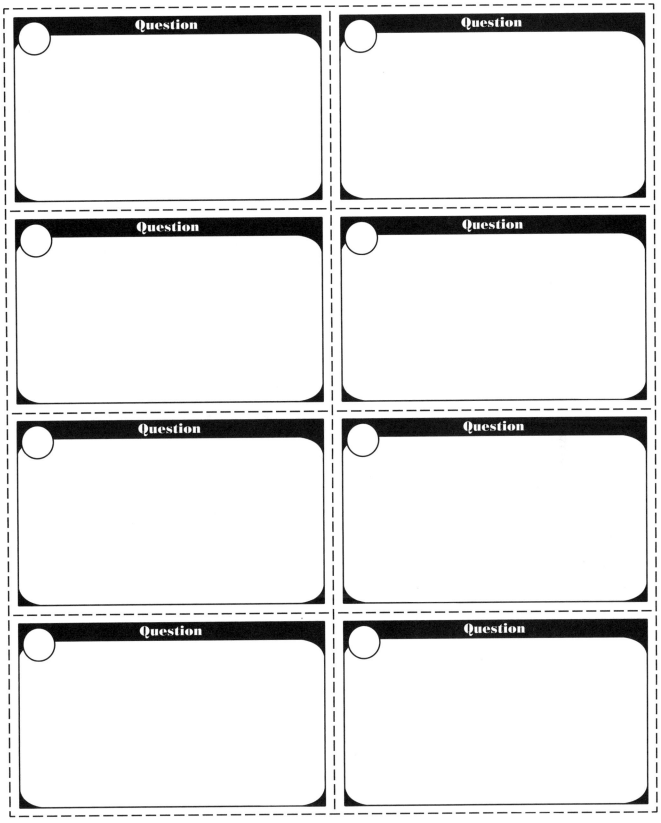

Simultaneous RoundTable

Structure 5

Structure 5

Simultaneous RoundTable

In teams, students each write a response on their own piece of paper. Students then pass their papers clockwise so each teammate can add another response or add on to the prior responses.

Group Size
Teams of Four

Steps

Setup: Each team of four needs four papers and four pencils.

 1 Teacher Assigns Topic
Teacher assigns a topic or question and provides think time.

 2 Students Respond
All four students respond, simultaneously writing, drawing, or answering questions.

 3 Teacher Signals Time's Up
The teacher signals time, or students place thumbs up when done with the problem.

 4 Students Pass Papers
Students pass papers or projects one person clockwise.

 5 Students Add to Papers
Students continue, adding to what was already completed.

 6 Repeat Process
Continue, starting at Step 3.

Tips
- Pass-N-Praise: Students are instructed not to release their paper until they receive a praiser that makes them feel good.

- Use four different worksheets. Students answer a problem, then pass it to a teammate to check and then answer the next problem.

Activities

Punctuation
Commas

Directions: For a team of four, hand out the four punctuation worksheets. Each teammate receives a different worksheet: 1) Commas, 2) Colons and Commas, 3) Quotation Marks, and 4) Caps and End Marks. Teammates correct the punctuation on the first sentence of their respective worksheet, then pass the worksheet clockwise. The next teammate checks the prior teammate's work, then corrects the next sentence. Teammates continue adding and passing until all worksheets are completed.

Punctuation Worksheet—Commas

1 She has final exams this week in her English history and biology courses.

2 The cook needed flour milk eggs chocolate chips and pecans to bake the cake.

3 Her presidential campaign was aggressive expensive and intense.

4 When you review the applicant's resume you will notice that he is highly qualified for the position.

5 Tell me Andrew where did you learn to sky dive?

6 Chapter 11 which contains the most detailed description was also the easiest to illustrate.

7 Residents in larger cities tend to travel using the city bus system local transit systems bicycles cabs or their own vehicles.

8 The movie we saw was funny sad exciting romantic and very realistic.

• Write
• Pass
• Check
  Teammate's
  work
• Write
• Pass

Punctuation
Colons and Commas

Directions: For a team of four, hand out the four punctuation worksheets. Each teammate receives a different worksheet: 1) Commas, 2) Colons and Commas, 3) Quotation Marks, and 4) Caps and End Marks. Teammates correct the punctuation on the first sentence of their respective worksheet, then pass the worksheet clockwise. The next teammate checks the prior teammate's work, then corrects the next sentence. Teammates continue adding and passing until all worksheets are completed.

Punctuation Worksheet—Colons and Commas

1. A delicious salad needs these ingredients lettuce carrots cucumbers tomatoes peppers and a tangy dressing.

2. Caution no life guard on duty.

3. The following teachers will be attending the meeting tomorrow Mr. Johnson Mr. North and Mr. Adams.

4. Most bikers need the same type of equipment bicycles helmets biking clothes helmet mirrors and a water bottle.

5. Be at my office promptly at 930 a.m.

6. Those going on the campout will need to bring these items a permission form a tent a sleeping bag and a campfire snack.

7. As a freshman I will take these core classes English biology American history and algebra.

8. While hiking in the Grand Canyon Paul suffered a sprained ankle sunburn splinters and even an allergy attack.

Simultaneous RoundTable

Blackline

Punctuation
Quotation Marks

- Write
- Pass
- Check Teammate's work
- Write
- Pass

Directions: For a team of four, hand out the four punctuation worksheets. Each teammate receives a different worksheet: 1) Commas, 2) Colons and Commas, 3) Quotation Marks, and 4) Caps and End Marks. Teammates correct the punctuation on the first sentence of their respective worksheet, then pass the worksheet clockwise. The next teammate checks the prior teammate's work, then corrects the next sentence. Teammates continue adding and passing until all worksheets are completed.

Punctuation Worksheet—Quotation Marks

(1) Who could deny her remarkable talents? questioned Alana.

(2) Did I actually hear her say, Is this a pop quiz?

(3) Alan suggested, Let's either have Italian or Mexican food for our evening meal.

(4) We wish this presidential election was over, said the campaign workers.

(5) One of my favorite old television programs is Perry Mason.

(6) Everyone will write a novel summary of chapter 14 as tomorrow's homework assignment, announced the teacher.

(7) Do you think it will work, asked Emily, to serve this menu at my birthday party?

(8) Let's order a large pepperoni pizza topped with extra cheese for tonight's dinner, suggested Beth.

Punctuation
Caps and End Marks

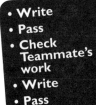

Directions: For a team of four, hand out the four punctuation worksheets. Each teammate receives a different worksheet: 1) Commas, 2) Colons and Commas, 3) Quotation Marks, and 4) Caps and End Marks. Teammates correct the punctuation on the first sentence of their respective worksheet, then pass the worksheet clockwise. The next teammate checks the prior teammate's work, then corrects the next sentence. Teammates continue adding and passing until all worksheets are completed.

Punctuation Worksheet—Caps and End Marks

1 ms. thomas, who was driving home from school that afternoon, said, "the car swerved right in front of me at the corner of payne and fairfield"

2 frank states, "i may have forgotten his name, but i'm sure i remember his face"

3 matt described his experiment as a "major disaster in motion" the other classmates heartily agreed

4 the soccer teams i'm rooting for in the world cup are germany, spain, and brazil do you think im being unpatriotic

5 certainly mr. franklin responded, i will explain the entire situation to him hopefully he will understand

6 no the mechanic stated curtly, i cannot get your vehicle repaired today

7 what did yogi berra mean when he said, "if you come to a fork in the road take it"

8 "im so excited" exclaimed beth "we haven't seen each other since texas at our trhs class reunion five years ago becky and heather are going to meet us at mama mia's italian ristorante

Punctuation
Answer Key

Punctuation Answer Key

Commas:

1. She has final exams this week in her English, history, and biology courses.

2. The cook needed flour, milk, eggs, chocolate chips, and pecans to bake the cake.

3. Her presidential campaign was aggressive, expensive, and intense.

4. When you review the applicant's resume, you will notice that he is highly qualified for the position.

5. Tell me, Andrew, where did you learn to sky dive?

6. Chapter 11, which contains the most detailed description, was also the easiest to illustrate.

7. Residents in larger cities tend to travel using the city bus system, local transit systems, bicycles, cabs, or their own vehicles.

8. The movie we saw was funny, sad, exciting, romantic, and very realistic.

Colons and Commas:

1. A delicious salad needs these ingredients: lettuce, carrots, cucumbers, tomatoes, peppers, and a tangy dressing.

2. Caution: no lifeguard on duty.

3. The following teachers will be attending the meeting tomorrow: Mr. Johnson, Mr. North, and Mr. Adams.

4. Most bikers need the same type of equipment: bicycles, helmets, biking clothes, helmet, mirrors, and a water bottle.

5. Be at my office promptly at 9:30 a.m.

6. Those going on the campout will need to bring these items: a permission form, a tent, a sleeping bag, and a campfire snack.

7. As a freshman I will take these core classes: English, biology, American history, and algebra.

8. While hiking in the Grand Canyon, Paul suffered a sprained ankle, sunburn, splinters, and even an allergy attack.

Punctuation
Answer Key

Punctuation Answer Key

Quotation Marks:

1. "Who could deny her remarkable talents?" questioned Alana.

2. Did I actually hear her say, "Is this a pop quiz?"

3. Alan suggested, "Let's either have Italian or Mexican food for our evening meal."

4. "We wish this presidential election was over," said the campaign workers.

5. One of my favorite old television programs is "Perry Mason."

6. "Everyone will write a novel summary of chapter 14 as tomorrow's homework assignment," announced the teacher.

7. "Do you think it will work," asked Emily, "to serve this menu at my birthday party?"

8. "Let's order a large pepperoni pizza topped with extra cheese for tonight's dinner," suggested Beth.

Caps and End Marks:

1. Ms. Thomas, who was driving home from school that afternoon, said, "The car swerved right in front of me at the corner of Payne and Fairfield."

2. Frank states, "I may have forgotten his name, but I'm sure I remember his face."

3. Matt described his experiment as "a major disaster in motion;" the other classmates heartily agreed.

4. The soccer teams I'm rooting for in the World Cup are Germany, Spain, and Brazil. Do you think I'm being unpatriotic?

5. "Certainly," Mr. Franklin responded, "I will explain the entire situation to him. Hopefully he will understand."

6. "No," the mechanic stated curtly, "I cannot get your vehicle repaired today."

7. What did Yogi Berra mean when he said, "If you come to a fork in the road, take it"?

8. "I'm so excited!" exclaimed Beth. "We haven't seen each other since Texas at our TRHS class reunion five years ago. Becky and Heather are going to meet us at Mama Mia's Italian Ristorante."

Antonyms and Synonyms

Directions: Each team receives four cards. Every team can have the same card set or each team may have unique sets. Teammates write a synonym or antonym on their cards and then pass the card clockwise. The next teammate checks the prior teammate's work, and then adds an answer. Teammates continue adding and passing until time is up.

Antonyms and Synonyms
Gaudy
Antonyms:
Synonyms:
Antonyms and Synonyms

Antonyms and Synonyms
Enthusiastic
Antonyms:
Synonyms:
Antonyms and Synonyms

Antonyms and Synonyms
Indifferent
Antonyms:
Synonyms:
Antonyms and Synonyms

Antonyms and Synonyms
Celebritiy
Antonyms:
Synonyms:
Antonyms and Synonyms

Antonyms and Synonyms *(continued)*

Directions: Each team receives four cards. Every team can have the same card set or each team may have unique sets. Teammates write a synonym or antonym on their cards and then pass the card clockwise. The next teammate checks the prior teammate's work, and then adds an answer. Teammates continue adding and passing until time is up.

Antonyms and Synonyms
Simple
Antonyms:
Synonyms:
Antonyms and Synonyms

Antonyms and Synonyms
Welcome
Antonyms:
Synonyms:
Antonyms and Synonyms

Antonyms and Synonyms
Airtight
Antonyms:
Synonyms:
Antonyms and Synonyms

Antonyms and Synonyms
Disperse
Antonyms:
Synonyms:
Antonyms and Synonyms

Antonyms and Synonyms (continued)

Directions: Each team receives four cards. Every team can have the same card set or each team may have unique sets. Teammates write a synonym or antonym on their cards and then pass the card clockwise. The next teammate checks the prior teammate's work, and then adds an answer. Teammates continue adding and passing until time is up.

Antonyms and Synonyms
Significant
Antonyms:
Synonyms:

Antonyms and Synonyms

Antonyms and Synonyms
Undermine
Antonyms:
Synonyms:

Antonyms and Synonyms

Antonyms and Synonyms
Commonplace
Antonyms:
Synonyms:

Antonyms and Synonyms

Antonyms and Synonyms
Reciprocal
Antonyms:
Synonyms:

Antonyms and Synonyms

Antonyms and Synonyms *(continued)*

Directions: Each team receives four cards. Every team can have the same card set or each team may have unique sets. Teammates write a synonym or antonym on their cards and then pass the card clockwise. The next teammate checks the prior teammate's work, and then adds an answer. Teammates continue adding and passing until time is up.

Antonyms and Synonyms
Elevated
Antonyms:
Synonyms:
Antonyms and Synonyms

Antonyms and Synonyms
Loyalist
Antonyms:
Synonyms:
Antonyms and Synonyms

Antonyms and Synonyms
Nullify
Antonyms:
Synonyms:
Antonyms and Synonyms

Antonyms and Synonyms
Vitality
Antonyms:
Synonyms:
Antonyms and Synonyms

Antonyms and Synonyms *(continued)*

Directions: Each team receives four cards. Every team can have the same card set or each team may have unique sets. Teammates write a synonym or antonym on their cards and then pass the card clockwise. The next teammate checks the prior teammate's work, and then adds an answer. Teammates continue adding and passing until time is up.

Antonyms and Synonyms
Firm
Antonyms:
Synonyms:
Antonyms and Synonyms

Antonyms and Synonyms
Exempt
Antonyms:
Synonyms:
Antonyms and Synonyms

Antonyms and Synonyms
Delusion
Antonyms:
Synonyms:
Antonyms and Synonyms

Antonyms and Synonyms
Nonchalant
Antonyms:
Synonyms:
Antonyms and Synonyms

Antonyms and Synonyms *(continued)*

Directions: Each team receives four cards. Every team can have the same card set or each team may have unique sets. Teammates write a synonym or antonym on their cards and then pass the card clockwise. The next teammate checks the prior teammate's work, and then adds an answer. Teammates continue adding and passing until time is up.

Antonyms and Synonyms
Morose
Antonyms:
Synonyms:
Antonyms and Synonyms

Antonyms and Synonyms
Naive
Antonyms:
Synonyms:
Antonyms and Synonyms

Antonyms and Synonyms
Pertinent
Antonyms:
Synonyms:
Antonyms and Synonyms

Antonyms and Synonyms
Cryptic
Antonyms:
Synonyms:
Antonyms and Synonyms

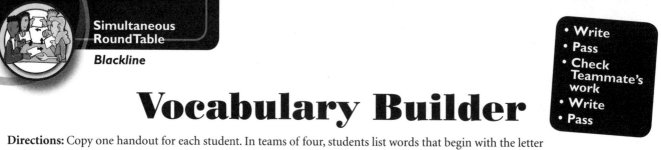

Simultaneous RoundTable

Blackline

- Write
- Pass
- Check Teammate's work
- Write
- Pass

Vocabulary Builder

Directions: Copy one handout for each student. In teams of four, students list words that begin with the letter at the front of the row. Words may relate to a recent reading assignment or topic. Students fill in as many words as possible in the allotted time given by the teacher and then pass worksheet clockwise. Teammates continue adding and passing until time is up.

Vocabulary Builder Worksheet

C	
H	
A	
R	
A	
C	
T	
E	
R	
S	

Types of Irony
Verbal Irony, Dramatic Irony, Situational Irony

TEACHER INSTRUCTIONS

Teams use Simultaneous RoundTable to define the types of irony and to list examples from texts.

1 Give students each a copy of the Types of Irony handout on page 154.

2 Explain to students how to fill out the worksheet. In the second column, students define the three types of irony: verbal irony, dramatic irony, and situational irony. In the third column, they provide an example of each type of irony from the text, along with a page number.

3 Have students begin filling out a worksheet.

4 Call "pass" after a minute or so. Students pass their papers clockwise to a teammate.

5 Teammates must check the worksheet and pick up where the prior teammate left off.

6 Call "pass" every few minutes until most teams have completed their worksheets.

Types of Irony Worksheet		
Types of Irony	**Definition**	**Example**
① Verbal Irony	What is said is the opposite of what is meant.	*Julius Caesar* "Yet Brutus says he was ambitious. And Brutus is an honourable man." Mark Antony says Brutus is an honorable man, but he really means that Brutus is a dishonorable man.
② Dramatic Irony	The reader grasps the truth, but the character thinks something different.	*Romeo and Juliet* Romeo discovers Juliet in a drugged sleep. He assumes she is dead and he kills himself. The reader knows she is not actually dead.
③ Situational Irony	The outcome turns out to be very different from what is expected.	*Macbeth* The witches predict something that will happen. It does happen although Macbeth often misinterprets their words about the happening.

Types of Irony

Directions: Fill out your worksheet until the teacher calls, "Pass." Pass your worksheet clockwise to your teammate. Inspect the worksheet you received and pick up where your teammate left off.

Types of Irony Worksheet		
Types of Irony	**Definition**	**Example**
① **Verbal Irony**		
② **Dramatic Irony**		
③ **Situational Irony**		

Simultaneous
Round Table

Blackline

Literary Devices

Directions: Fill out your worksheet until the teacher calls, "Pass." Pass your worksheet clockwise to your teammate. Inspect the worksheet you received and pick up where your teammate left off.

Literary Devices Worksheet

Literary Devices	Definition	Example
1 Flashback		
2 Foreshadowing		
3 Irony		
4 Symbolism		

Novel Study
Hard Times by Charles Dickens

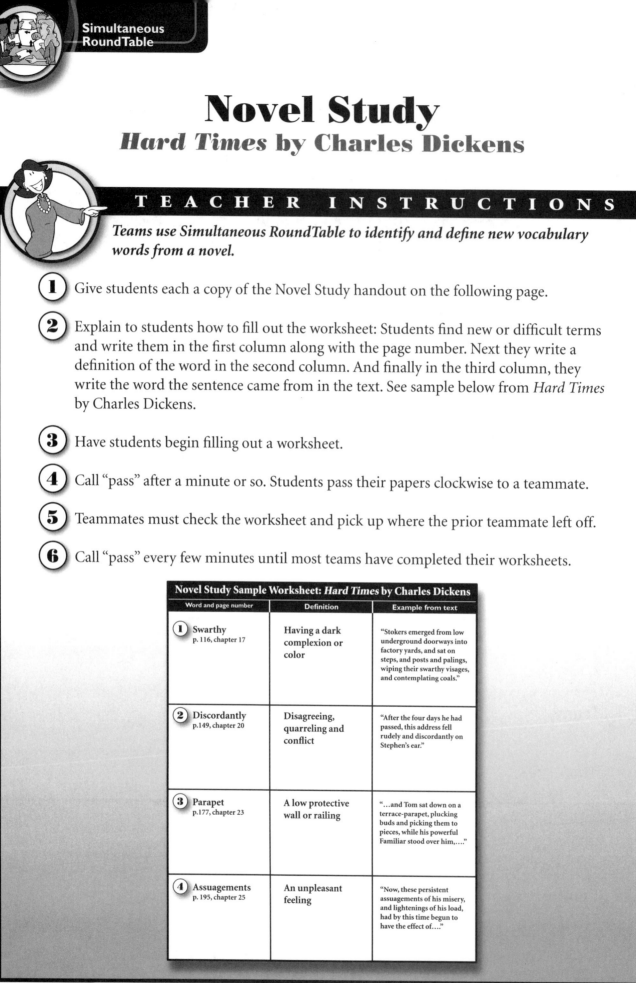

T E A C H E R   I N S T R U C T I O N S

Teams use Simultaneous RoundTable to identify and define new vocabulary words from a novel.

1 Give students each a copy of the Novel Study handout on the following page.

2 Explain to students how to fill out the worksheet: Students find new or difficult terms and write them in the first column along with the page number. Next they write a definition of the word in the second column. And finally in the third column, they write the word the sentence came from in the text. See sample below from *Hard Times* by Charles Dickens.

3 Have students begin filling out a worksheet.

4 Call "pass" after a minute or so. Students pass their papers clockwise to a teammate.

5 Teammates must check the worksheet and pick up where the prior teammate left off.

6 Call "pass" every few minutes until most teams have completed their worksheets.

Novel Study Sample Worksheet: *Hard Times* by Charles Dickens

Word and page number	Definition	Example from text
1 Swarthy p. 116, chapter 17	Having a dark complexion or color	"Stokers emerged from low underground doorways into factory yards, and sat on steps, and posts and palings, wiping their swarthy visages, and contemplating coals."
2 Discordantly p.149, chapter 20	Disagreeing, quarreling and conflict	"After the four days he had passed, this address fell rudely and discordantly on Stephen's ear."
3 Parapet p.177, chapter 23	A low protective wall or railing	"…and Tom sat down on a terrace-parapet, plucking buds and picking them to pieces, while his powerful Familiar stood over him,…."
4 Assuagements p. 195, chapter 25	An unpleasant feeling	"Now, these persistent assuagements of his misery, and lightenings of his load, had by this time begun to have the effect of…."

- Write
- Pass
- Check Teammate's work
- Write
- Pass

Novel Study
Words from the Text

Directions: Fill out your worksheet until the teacher calls, "Pass." Pass your worksheet clockwise to your teammate. Inspect the worksheet you received and pick up where your teammate left off.

Words from the Text Worksheet		
Word and page number	**Definition**	**Example from text**

Thinking Questions
Any Novel

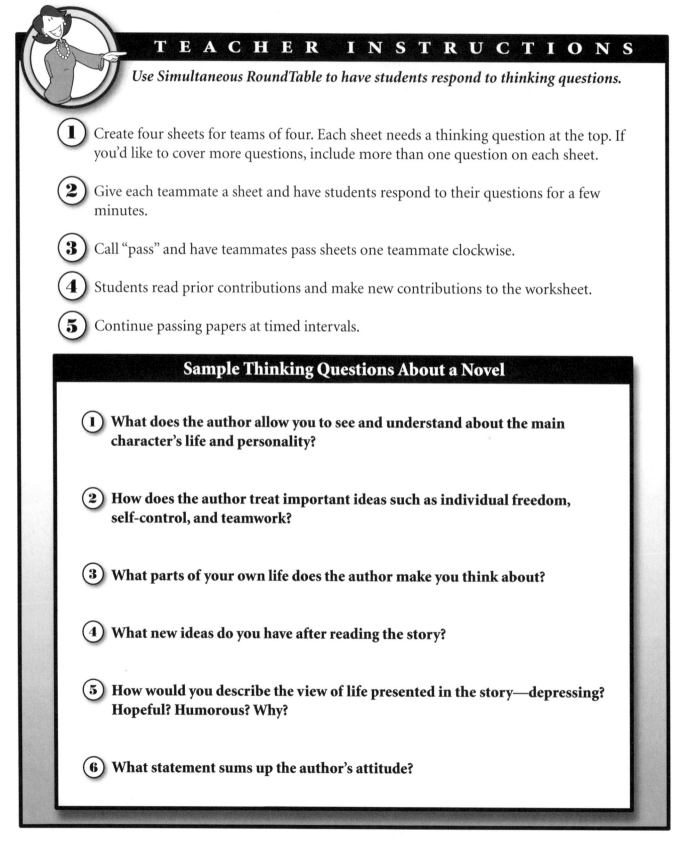

TEACHER INSTRUCTIONS

Use Simultaneous RoundTable to have students respond to thinking questions.

1 Create four sheets for teams of four. Each sheet needs a thinking question at the top. If you'd like to cover more questions, include more than one question on each sheet.

2 Give each teammate a sheet and have students respond to their questions for a few minutes.

3 Call "pass" and have teammates pass sheets one teammate clockwise.

4 Students read prior contributions and make new contributions to the worksheet.

5 Continue passing papers at timed intervals.

Sample Thinking Questions About a Novel

1 What does the author allow you to see and understand about the main character's life and personality?

2 How does the author treat important ideas such as individual freedom, self-control, and teamwork?

3 What parts of your own life does the author make you think about?

4 What new ideas do you have after reading the story?

5 How would you describe the view of life presented in the story—depressing? Hopeful? Humorous? Why?

6 What statement sums up the author's attitude?

Literature
Graphic Organizers

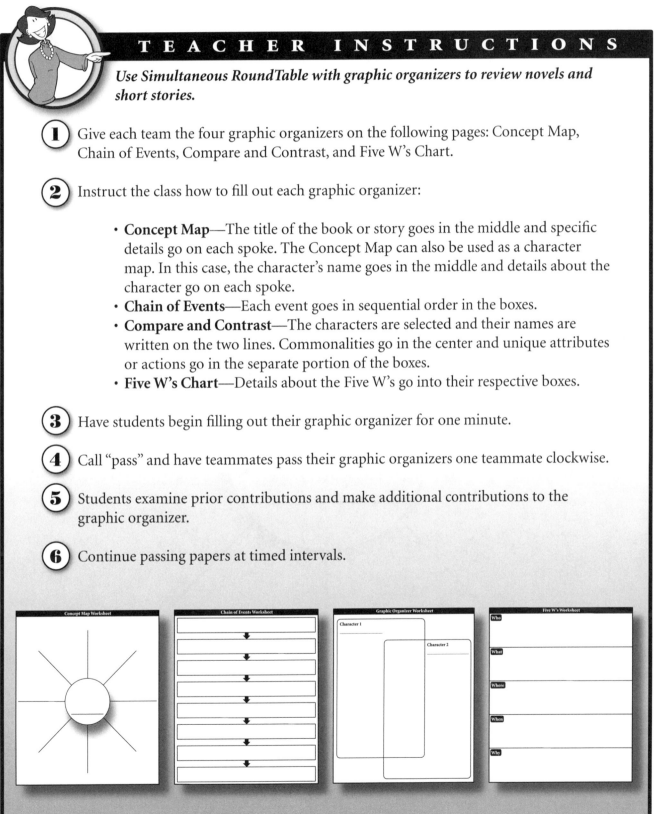

T E A C H E R I N S T R U C T I O N S

Use Simultaneous RoundTable with graphic organizers to review novels and short stories.

1 Give each team the four graphic organizers on the following pages: Concept Map, Chain of Events, Compare and Contrast, and Five W's Chart.

2 Instruct the class how to fill out each graphic organizer:

- **Concept Map**—The title of the book or story goes in the middle and specific details go on each spoke. The Concept Map can also be used as a character map. In this case, the character's name goes in the middle and details about the character go on each spoke.
- **Chain of Events**—Each event goes in sequential order in the boxes.
- **Compare and Contrast**—The characters are selected and their names are written on the two lines. Commonalities go in the center and unique attributes or actions go in the separate portion of the boxes.
- **Five W's Chart**—Details about the Five W's go into their respective boxes.

3 Have students begin filling out their graphic organizer for one minute.

4 Call "pass" and have teammates pass their graphic organizers one teammate clockwise.

5 Students examine prior contributions and make additional contributions to the graphic organizer.

6 Continue passing papers at timed intervals.

Concept Map
Graphic Organizer

• Write
• Pass
• Check Teammate's work
• Write
• Pass

Directions: Fill in information on this graphic organizer until time is up. Pass your worksheet clockwise. Look over your new worksheet before adding new information.

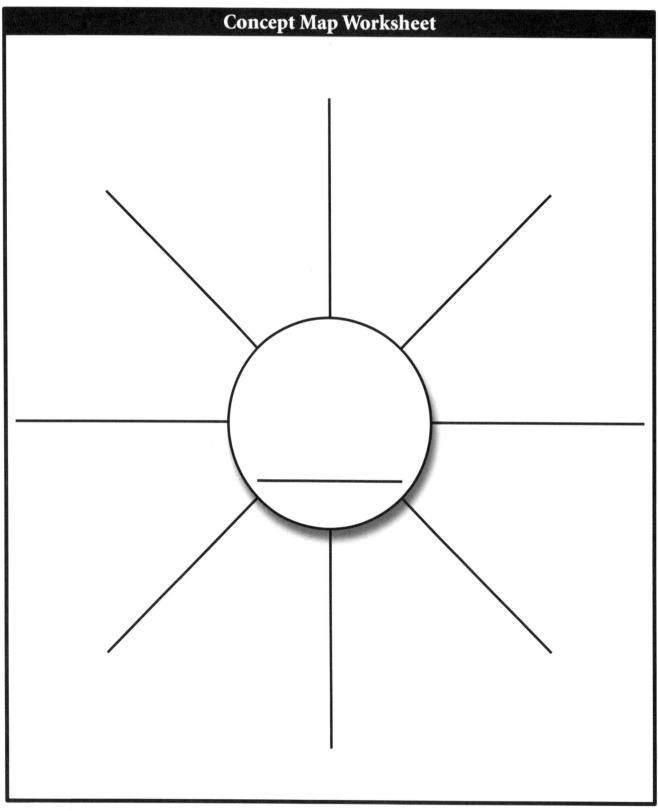

Concept Map Worksheet

Chain of Events
Graphic Organizer

Directions: Fill in information on this graphic organizer until time is up. Pass your worksheet clockwise. Look over your new worksheet before adding new information.

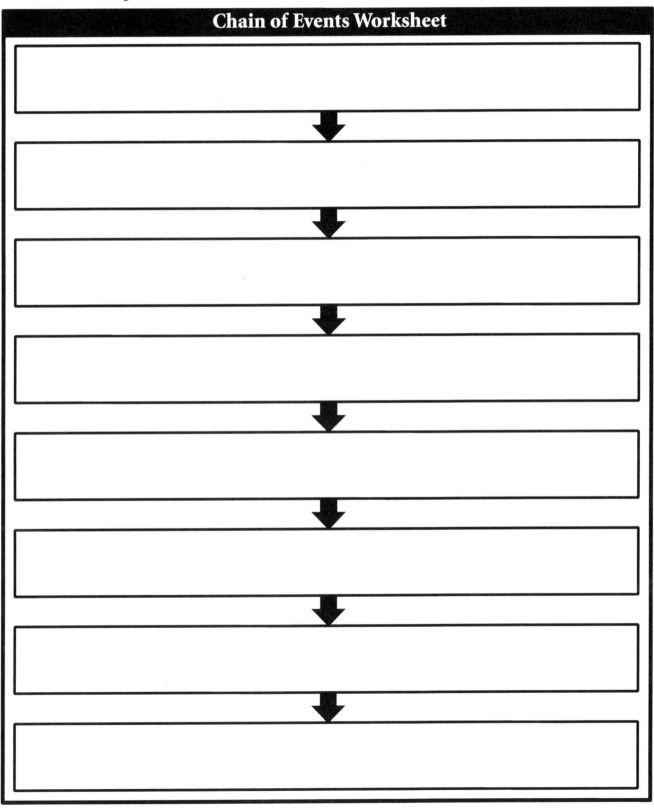

Chain of Events Worksheet

Simultaneous
RoundTable

Blackline

• Write
• Pass
• Check
  Teammate's
  work
• Write
• Pass

Compare and Contrast
Venn Diagram Graphic Organizer

Directions: Fill in information on this graphic organizer until time is up. Pass your worksheet clockwise. Look over your new worksheet before adding new information.

Graphic Organizer Worksheet

Character 1

_____

Character 2

_____

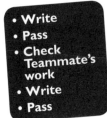
- Write
- Pass
- Check Teammate's work
- Write
- Pass

Five W's Chart
Graphic Organizer

Directions: Fill in information on this graphic organizer until time is up. Pass your worksheet clockwise. Look over your new worksheet before adding new information.

Five W's Worksheet

Who

What

Where

When

Why

Team Word-Webbing

Structure 6

Structure 6

Team Word-Webbing

Students each write in their own color on a team word-web, which includes a main idea, core concepts, supporting details, and bridges.

Group Size
Teams of Four

Steps

Setup: Each team receives a large sheet of butcher paper and a different color marker for each teammate.

1 **Teacher States Idea**
Teacher announces the main idea.

2 **Teammate Records Main Idea**
One teammate writes the main idea in the center of the team paper and draws a rectangle around it.

3 **Teammates Write Core Concepts**
Teammates RoundTable core concepts. Core concepts are written in ovals connected by lines to the main idea.

4 **Free-for-All**
The team has a free-for-all. In his or her unique color, teammates write details and draw bridges between related ideas.

Variation: The teacher may provide the core concepts instead of having students generate their own. This provides more guidance for the word-web. The blacklines in this section include the core concepts.

Tips
- Give teams time to discuss and improve their webs.
- Consider a class discussion on the topic.
- Have teams post their webs for other teams to review.
- Use the web for individual writing assignments on the topic.
- Teams can copy the blacklines provided onto butcher paper for larger word webs.

Activities

Word-Web
Blank Template...180

Vocabulary
Word-Web

Directions: As a team, fill in the meaning of the word, synonyms, antonyms, and context examples.

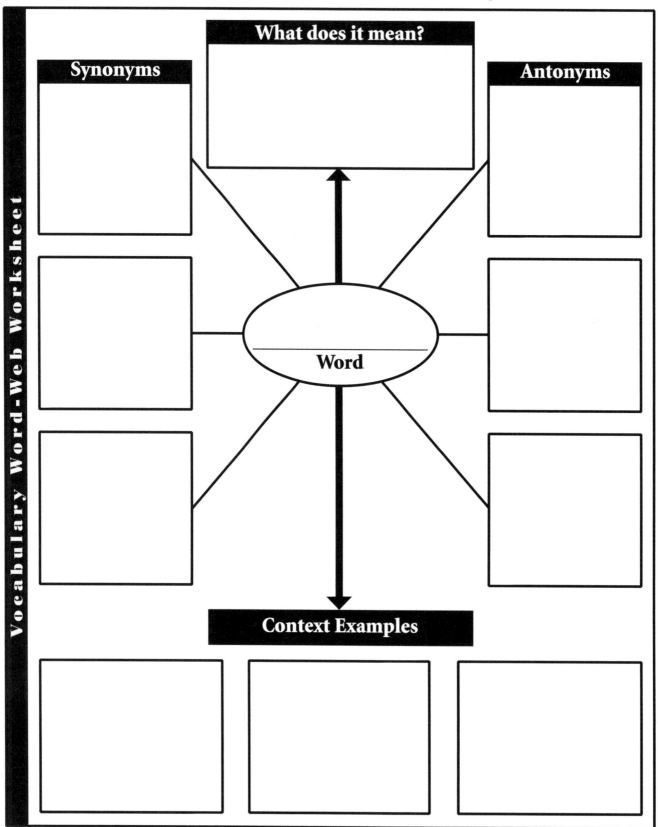

Vocabulary Word-Web Worksheet

What does it mean?

Synonyms

Antonyms

Word

Context Examples

Character
Word-Web

Directions: As a team, add details to this word web. Make connections between related ideas.

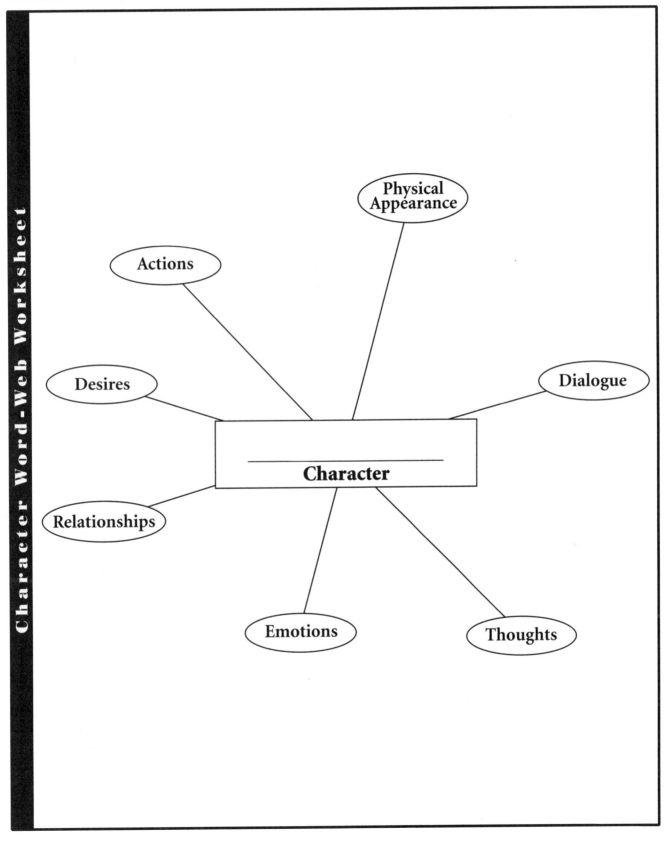

Character Word-Web Worksheet

Physical Appearance

Actions

Desires

Dialogue

Relationships

Character

Emotions

Thoughts

Figurative Language
Word-Web

Directions: As a team, add details to this word web. Make connections between related ideas.

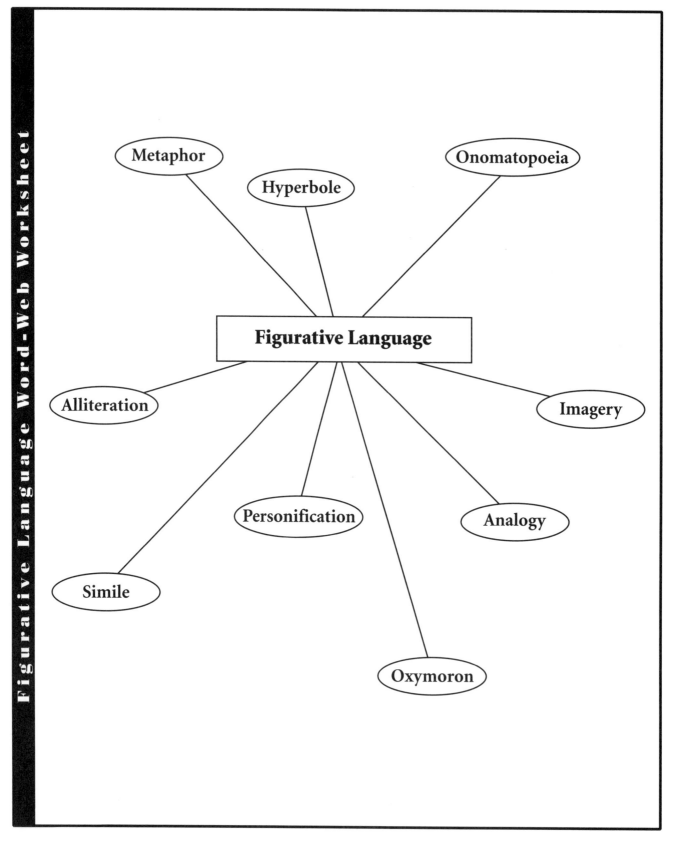

Story Elements
Word-Web

Directions: As a team, add details to this word web. Make connections between related ideas.

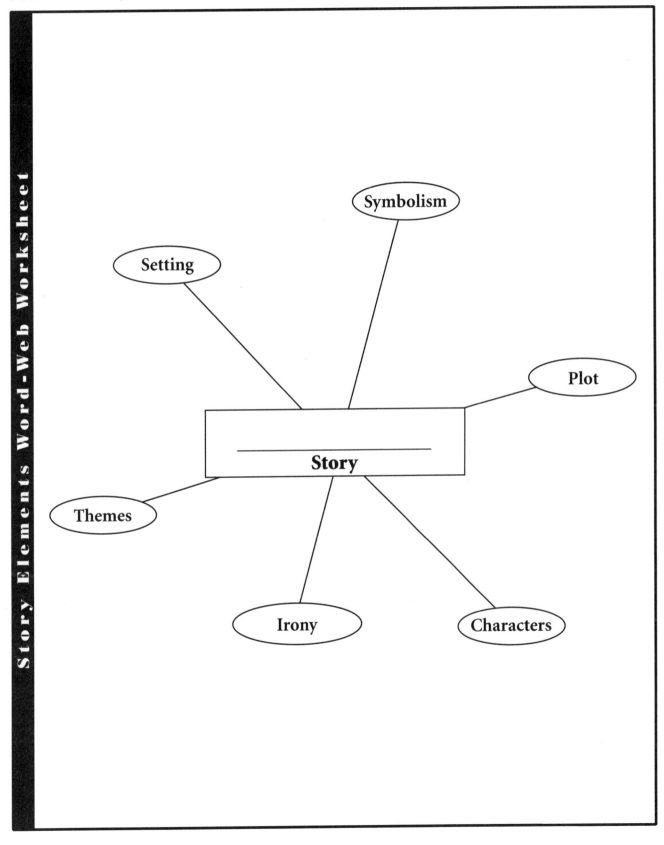

Parts of Speech
Word-Web

Directions: As a team, add details to this word web. Make connections between related ideas.

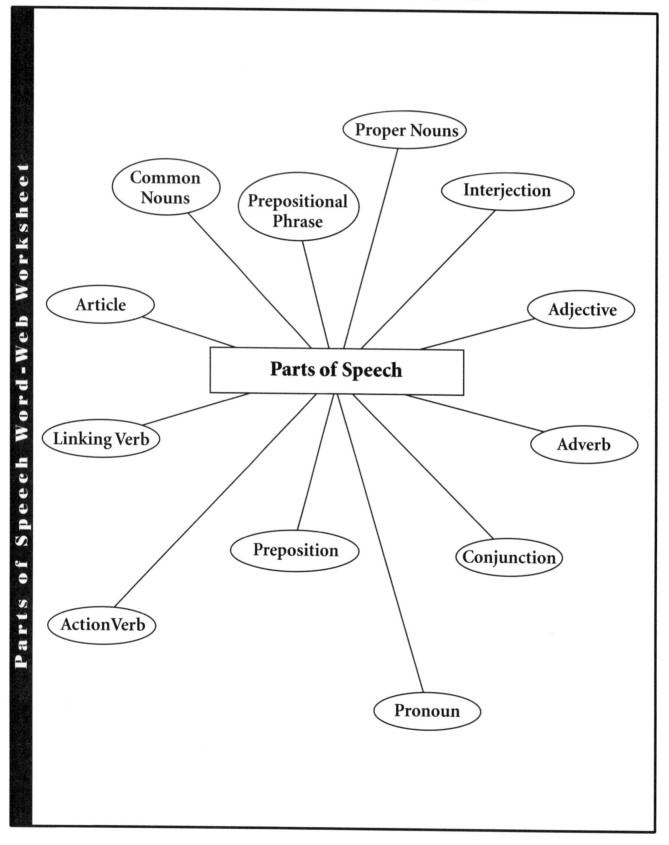

Parts of Speech Word-Web Worksheet

Proper Nouns

Common Nouns

Prepositional Phrase

Interjection

Article

Adjective

Parts of Speech

Linking Verb

Adverb

Preposition

Conjunction

ActionVerb

Pronoun

Punctuation
Word-Web

Directions: As a team, add details to this word web. Make connections between related ideas.

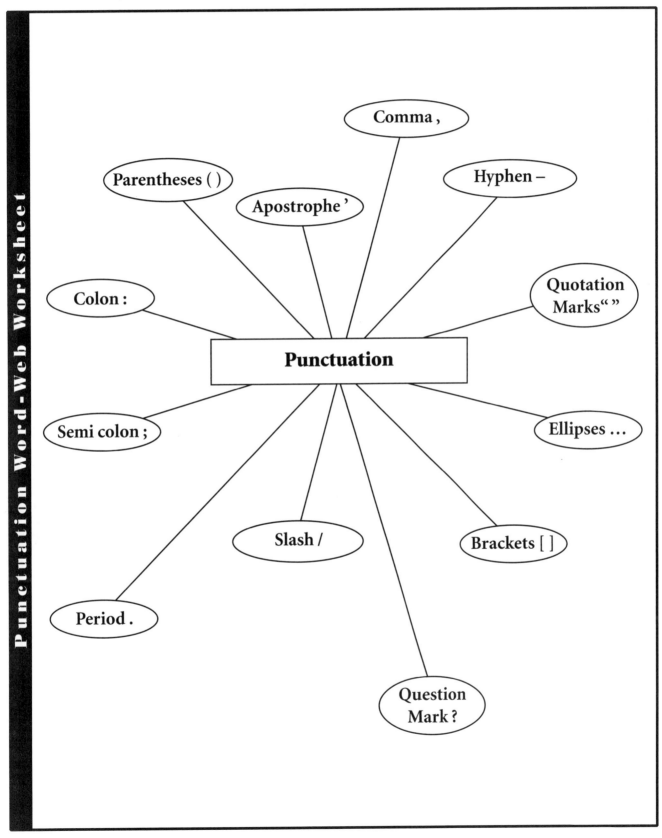

Punctuation Word-Web Worksheet

- Comma ,
- Parentheses ( )
- Apostrophe '
- Hyphen –
- Quotation Marks " "
- Colon :
- **Punctuation**
- Semi colon ;
- Ellipses …
- Slash /
- Brackets [ ]
- Period .
- Question Mark ?

Literary Periods
Word-Web

Directions: As a team, add details to this word web. Make connections between related ideas.

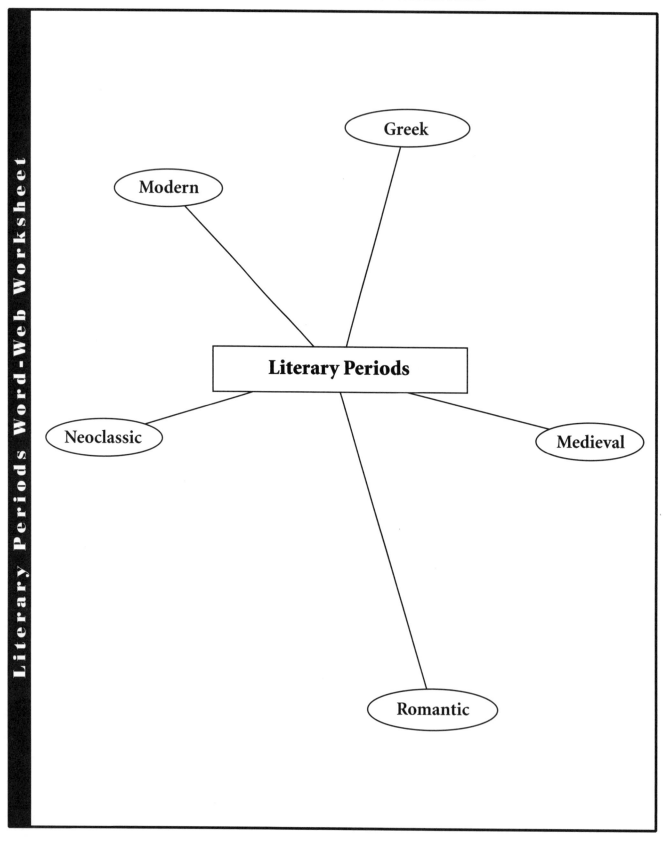

Greek

Modern

Literary Periods

Neoclassic

Medieval

Romantic

Poetry
Word-Web

Directions: As a team, add details to this word web. Make connections between related ideas.

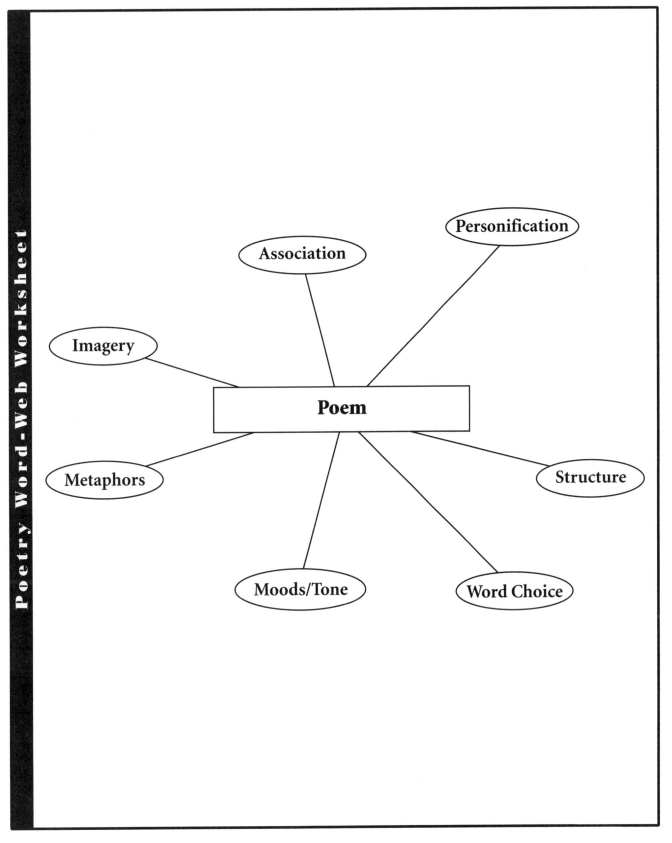

Julius Caesar
Act and Scene Word-Web

Directions: As a team, add details to this word web. Make connections between related ideas.

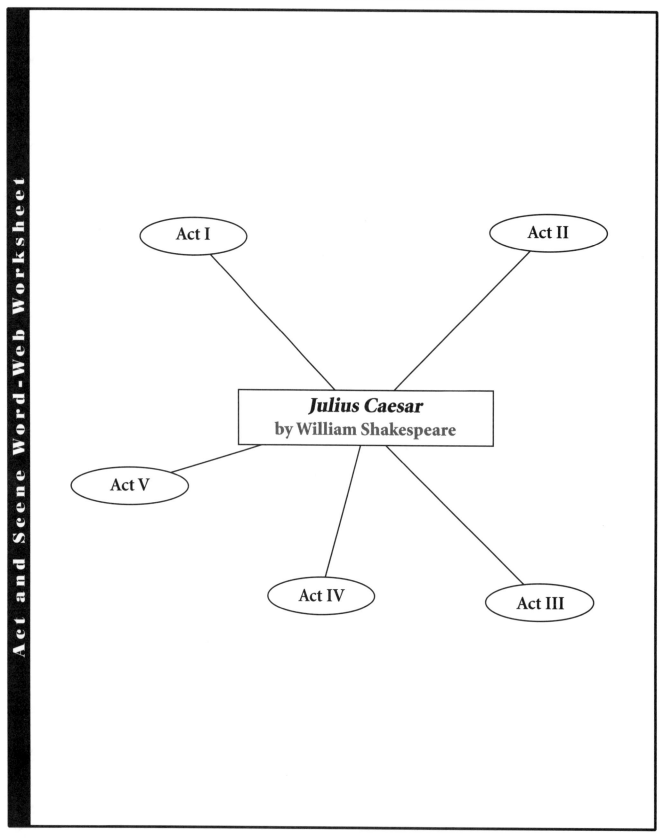

Act and Scene Word-Web Worksheet

Act I

Act II

Julius Caesar
by William Shakespeare

Act V

Act IV

Act III

The Grapes of Wrath
Blackline
Master Themes Word-Web

Directions: As a team, add details to this word web. Make connections between related ideas.

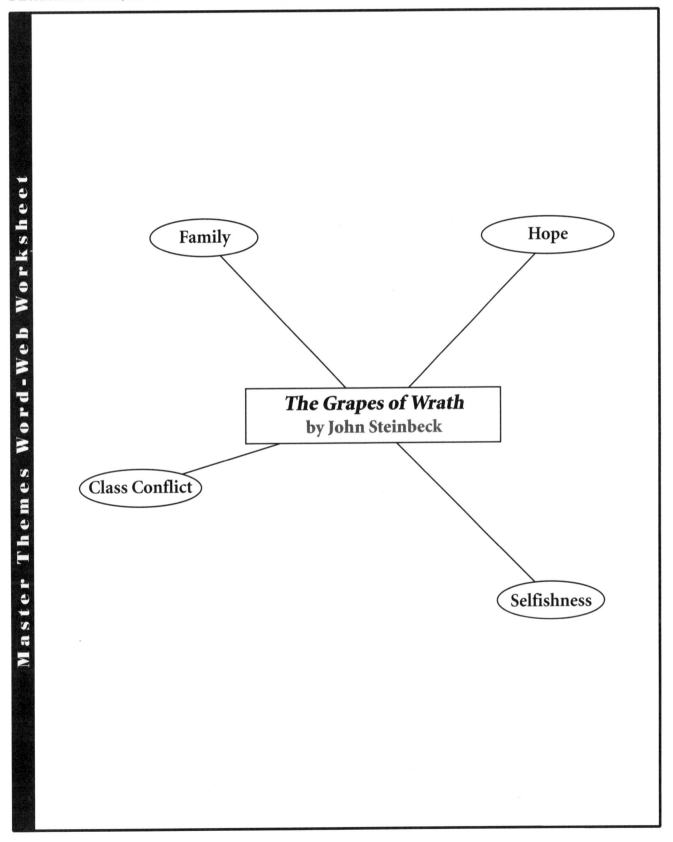

Family

Hope

The Grapes of Wrath
by John Steinbeck

Class Conflict

Selfishness

Master Themes Word-Web Worksheet

Catch–22
Character Word-Web

Directions: As a team, add details to this word web. Make connections between related ideas.

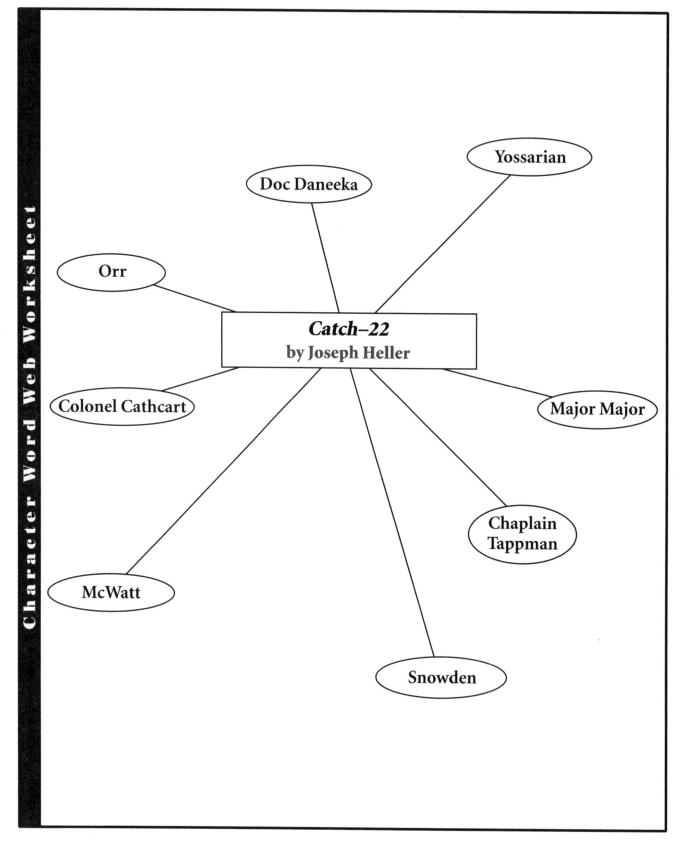

Character Word Web Worksheet

Doc Daneeka

Yossarian

Orr

Catch–22
by Joseph Heller

Colonel Cathcart

Major Major

Chaplain Tappman

McWatt

Snowden

William Shakespeare
Word-Web

Directions: As a team, add details to this word web. Make connections between related ideas.

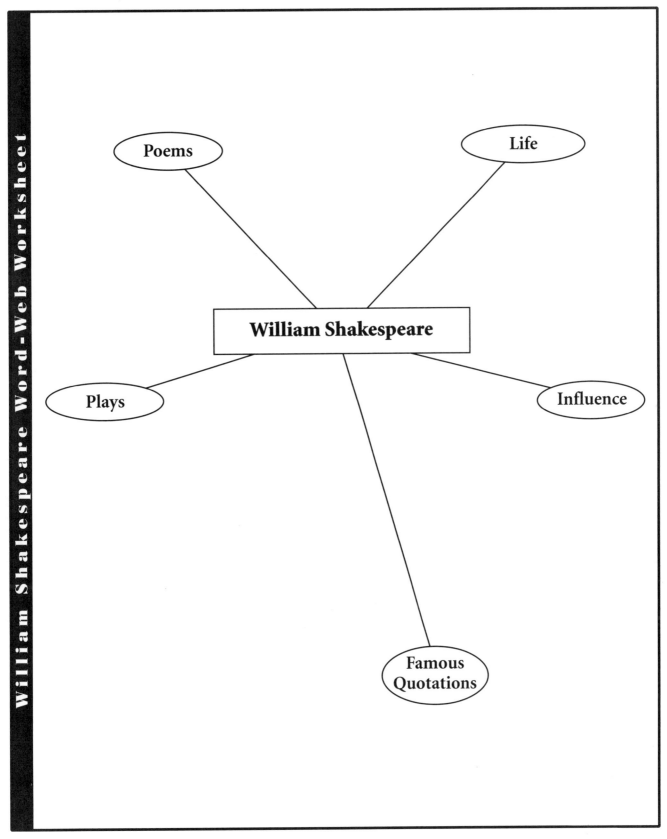

Poems

Life

William Shakespeare

Plays

Influence

Famous Quotations

William Shakespeare Word-Web Worksheet

Blank Template
Word-Web

Directions: Use this worksheet to do Team Word-Webbing on any topic.

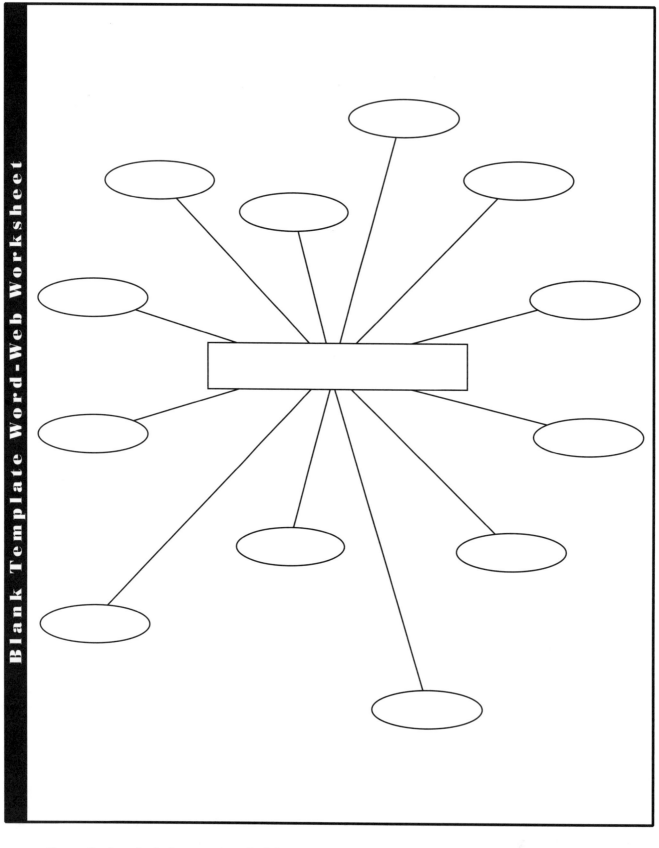

Think-Write-RoundRobin

Structure 7

Think-Write-RoundRobin

Students take turns sharing their writing with teammates.

Group Size
Teams of Four

Steps

Setup: Each student needs a piece of paper and pen.

1 Teacher Assigns Task
Teacher presents a question or assigns a writing task. For example, *"Which sonnet do you prefer and why?"*

2 Think Time
Teacher provides students think time to think of their responses.

3 Students Write
Students write their responses.

4 Students Share
Students share their writing with their teammates, using RoundRobin. The student selected stands and reads first, then sits when done. The next teammate on his or her left stands to share next, and so on.

Tips
- Use a random selector to select a student to share first in the RoundRobin.
- Have students stand to share. When all students are seated, you know everyone is done.
- Students may write on multiple topics or questions and share in multiple rounds of RoundRobin.

Activities

**Think-Write-RoundRobin
Blank Worksheet...196**

The Great Gatsby
Analyzing Quotes

Directions: Read the quotes below. Independently write the context of the quote and what each quote means. Then, team up and share in turn your interpretation of the quote. You may record additional ideas from teammates as they share.

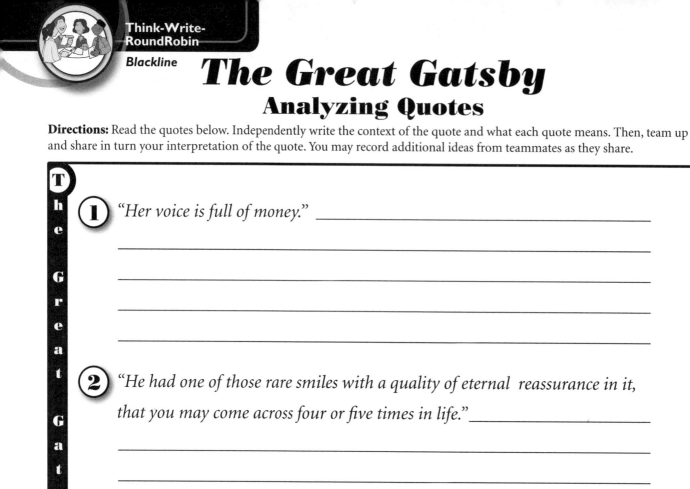

The Great Gatsby Quotes Worksheet

1 *"Her voice is full of money."* _____

_____

_____

_____

_____

2 *"He had one of those rare smiles with a quality of eternal reassurance in it, that you may come across four or five times in life."* _____

_____

_____

_____

_____

3 *"This is a valley of ashes—a fantastic farm where ashes grow like wheat...."*

_____

_____

_____

_____

4 *"Reserving judgments is a matter of infinite hope."* _____

_____

_____

_____

_____

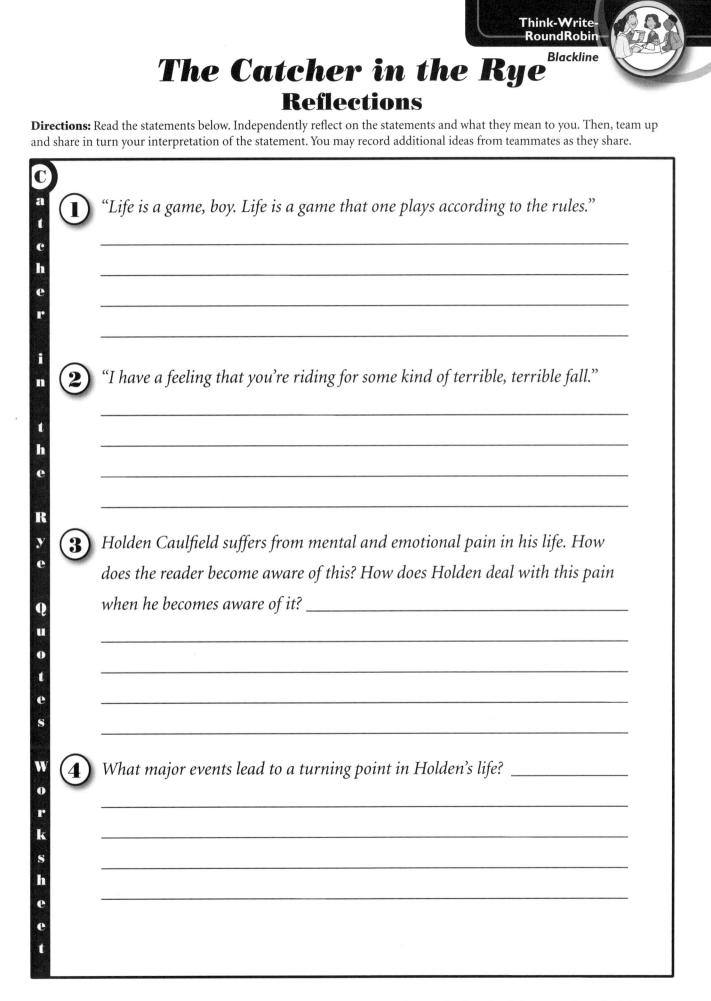

The Catcher in the Rye
Reflections

Directions: Read the statements below. Independently reflect on the statements and what they mean to you. Then, team up and share in turn your interpretation of the statement. You may record additional ideas from teammates as they share.

Catcher in the Rye Quotes Worksheet

① *"Life is a game, boy. Life is a game that one plays according to the rules."*

_____

_____

_____

_____

② *"I have a feeling that you're riding for some kind of terrible, terrible fall."*

_____

_____

_____

③ *Holden Caulfield suffers from mental and emotional pain in his life. How does the reader become aware of this? How does Holden deal with this pain when he becomes aware of it?* _____

_____

_____

_____

④ *What major events lead to a turning point in Holden's life?* _____

_____

_____

_____

The Pearl
Predicting Meaning Before Reading

Directions: Read the quotes below. Independently write the context of the quote and what each quote means. Then, team up and share in turn your interpretation of the quote. You may record additional ideas from teammates as they share.

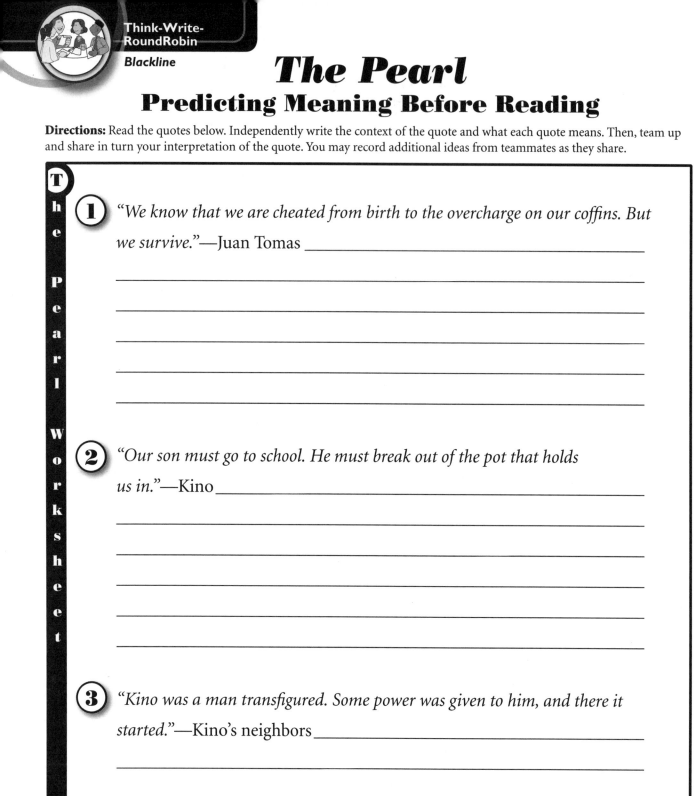

1 *"We know that we are cheated from birth to the overcharge on our coffins. But we survive."*—Juan Tomas _____

_____

_____

_____

_____

_____

2 *"Our son must go to school. He must break out of the pot that holds us in."*—Kino _____

_____

_____

_____

_____

_____

3 *"Kino was a man transfigured. Some power was given to him, and there it started."*—Kino's neighbors _____

_____

_____

_____

_____

_____

The Pearl
Predicting Meaning Before Reading *(continued)*

Directions: Read the quotes below. Independently write the context of the quote and what each quote means. Then, team up and share in turn your interpretation of the quote. You may record additional ideas from teammates as they share.

The Pearl Worksheet

4 *"This pearl has become my soul. If I give it up I shall lose my soul."*—Kino

_____

_____

_____

_____

_____

5 *"Have I nothing better to do than cure insect bites for 'little Indians'? I am a doctor, not a veterinarian."* —the doctor _____

_____

_____

_____

_____

_____

6 *"My son will read and open books, and my son will write and know writing. And my son will make numbers, and these things will make us free because he will know—he will know and through him we will know."* —Kino_____

_____

_____

_____

_____

_____

The Great Gatsby
Symbolism

Use Think-Write-RoundRobin to have students brainstorm symbolism used in the novel, The Great Gatsby, *then share their examples with teammates.*

1 Call out a symbol from the list below.

2 Have students think, then write what the phrase symbolized in the novel, *The Great Gatsby,* on a slip of paper or response board.

3 Using RoundRobin, have each teammate in turn read what he or she wrote about the symbol. Students can record additional ideas as their teammates share.

4 Repeat with the next symbol.

The Great Gatsby Symbols

- **Valley of ashes**
- **The mantle clock**
- **The eyes of Dr. Eckleburg**
- **The green light**
- **The owl-eyed man**

Prefixes

Use Think-Write-RoundRobin to have students brainstorm words that begin with a given prefix, then share their examples with teammates.

1 Call out a prefix from the list of prefixes below.

2 Have students think, then write words that begin with the prefix on a slip of paper or response board.

3 Using RoundRobin, have each teammate in turn share his or her words that use the given prefix. Students can record additional words their teammates share.

4 Repeat with the next prefix.

Prefixes to Use

non-	**sub-**	**dec-**
pre-	**pre-**	**tri-**
tri-	**co-**	**inter-**
dis-	**ultra-**	**macro-**
non-	**post-**	**circum-**
re-	**trans-**	
dis-	**ante-**	

Suffixes

Use Think-Write-RoundRobin to have students brainstorm words that begin with a given suffix, then share their examples with teammates.

1 Call out a suffix from the list of suffixes below.

2 Have students think, then write words that begin with the suffix on a slip of paper or response board.

3 Using RoundRobin, have each teammate in turn share his or her words that use the given suffix. Students can record additional words their teammates share.

4 Repeat with the next suffix.

Suffixes to Use

-ment	-ation
-tion	-ment
-ity	-ion
-fy	-fy, -ify
-ible	-ty, -ity
-able	-tion

Word Definitions 1

Directions: Define each term in your own words. Identify the origin of the root word. Then team up and share your definition in turn with teammates. You may modify your definition, based on feedback from teammates.

W
o
r
d

D
e
f
i
n
i
t
i
o
n
s

W
o
r
k
s
h
e
e
t

(1) Actor _____ | Origin |

(2) Bibliography _____ | Origin |

(3) Inference _____ | Origin |

(4) Cryptic_____ | Origin |

(5) Hydraulic_____ | Origin |

(6) Project _____ | Origin |

(7) Subscribe _____ | Origin |

(8) Contract_____ | Origin |

(9) Revert_____ | Origin |

Word Definitions 2

Directions: Define each term in your own words. Identify the origin of the root word. Then team up and share your definition in turn with teammates. You may modify your definition, based on feedback from teammates.

W o r d   D e f i n i t i o n s   W o r k s h e e t

(1) Capital _____ | Origin |

_____

_____

(2) Transpose _____ | Origin |

_____

_____

(3) Reconstruct _____ | Origin |

_____

_____

(4) Monarch _____ | Origin |

_____

_____

(5) Demographic _____ | Origin |

_____

_____

(6) Geology _____ | Origin |

_____

_____

(7) Dictate _____ | Origin |

_____

_____

(8) Metropolis _____ | Origin |

_____

_____

(9) Technology _____ | Origin |

_____

_____

Character Chart
A Lesson Before Dying

Directions: Complete the column on the first character in the chart. When done, team up and take turns sharing your responses with teammates. You may add teammates' ideas that you like. After sharing, move on to the next character.

Character Chart Worksheet		Grant	Jefferson	Tante Lou	Miss Emma	Reverend Ambrose
	Character's Words/Actions					
	Thoughts					
	Appearance					
	What others think of the character					

Reading Strategy
Before Reading

Directions: Before reading a novel, fill in your responses to the following prompts. Then, team up and share your responses in turn with teammates. Record your teammates' ideas as they share them.

Reading Strategy Before Reading

Predict	Question
I predict…	I'm wondering…
My teammates predict…	My teammates wonder…

Visualize	Conclusions
I imagine…	I think…
My teammates imagine…	My teammates think…

Reading Strategy
After Reading

Directions: After reading a novel, fill in your responses to the following prompts. Then, team up and share your responses in turn with teammates. Record your teammates' ideas as they share them.

Predict	Question
My prediction was…	I discovered…
My teammates' prediction was…	My teammates discovered…

Visualize	Conclusions
Now I picture…	My conclusion after reading…
Now my teammates picture…	My teammates' conclusion after reading…

Think-Write-RoundRobin
Blank Worksheet

Directions: Use this form to do Think-Write-RoundRobin on any topic. Fill in the topic in the Think box below.

T h i n k - W r i t e - R o u n d R o b i n   W o r k s h e e t

Think Think about your response to the following: _____

_____

_____

_____

_____

_____

_____

Write Write your response. Be ready to read your response to teammates. _____

_____

_____

_____

_____

_____

_____

_____

_____

_____

_____

_____

_____

_____

RoundRobin Use this space to record ideas you hear from teammates as they share.

_____

_____

_____

_____

_____

Timed Pair Share
Structure 8

Structure 8
Timed Pair Share

The teacher provides a discussion topic. In pairs, students share with a partner for a predetermined time while the partner listens. Then partners switch roles.

Group Size
Pairs

1 **Teacher Asks Question**
The teacher asks a question that students may elaborate on and provides think time. *"What is Twain's position on slavery? Think time."*

2 **Partner A Shares**
In pairs, Partner A shares while Partner B listens without talking. *"Partner A, please share your response for 30 seconds. Partner B, you are listening carefully, no talking."*

3 **Partner B Responds**
The teacher tells Partner B how to respond. The response can be simply to copycat the teacher's response:

• *Thanks for sharing!*
• *You are simply fascinating to listen to!*
The response can be to complete a sentence starter such as:
• *One thing I learned listening to you was…*
• *I enjoyed listening to you because…*
Or the response can be a spontaneous response by the listener.

4 **Switch Roles**
Partners switch roles. Partner B shares while Partner A listens, then Partner A responds.

Tips
• Let students know who will be Partner A and Partner B.
• Use a random selector to pick who will go first, Partner A or Partner B.
• Use fun prompts to decide who will go first such as "the student who is closer to the ceiling goes first."

Activities

**Question Cards
Blank Template...208**

Any Novel
Question Cards

Directions: Copy enough cards so each student receives a Question Card. Have students stand up, pair up, and do Timed Pair Share to respond to each other's questions. Students trade cards and find a new partner to share.

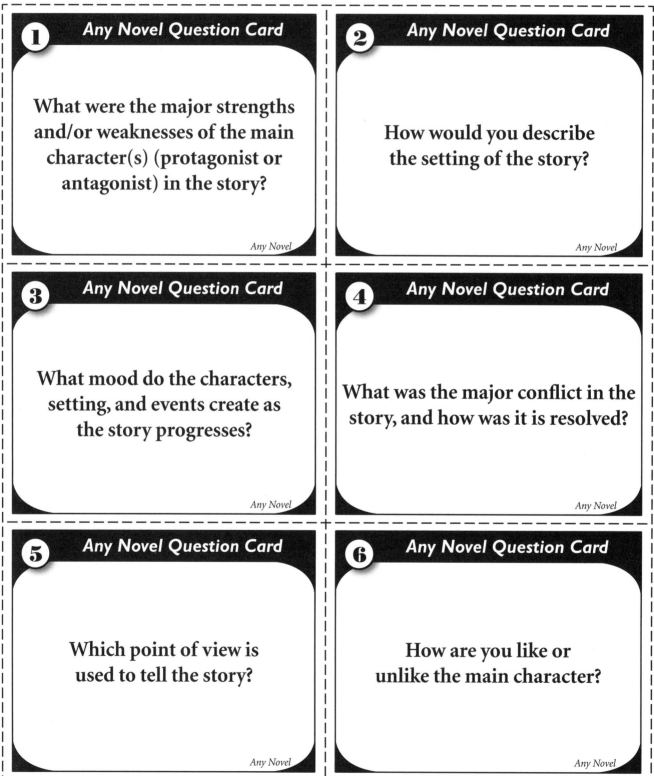

① Any Novel Question Card

What were the major strengths and/or weaknesses of the main character(s) (protagonist or antagonist) in the story?

Any Novel

② Any Novel Question Card

How would you describe the setting of the story?

Any Novel

③ Any Novel Question Card

What mood do the characters, setting, and events create as the story progresses?

Any Novel

④ Any Novel Question Card

What was the major conflict in the story, and how was it is resolved?

Any Novel

⑤ Any Novel Question Card

Which point of view is used to tell the story?

Any Novel

⑥ Any Novel Question Card

How are you like or unlike the main character?

Any Novel

Any Novel
Question Cards *(continued)*

Directions: Copy enough cards so each student receives a Question Card. Have students stand up, pair up, and do Timed Pair Share to respond to each other's questions. Students trade cards and find a new partner to share.

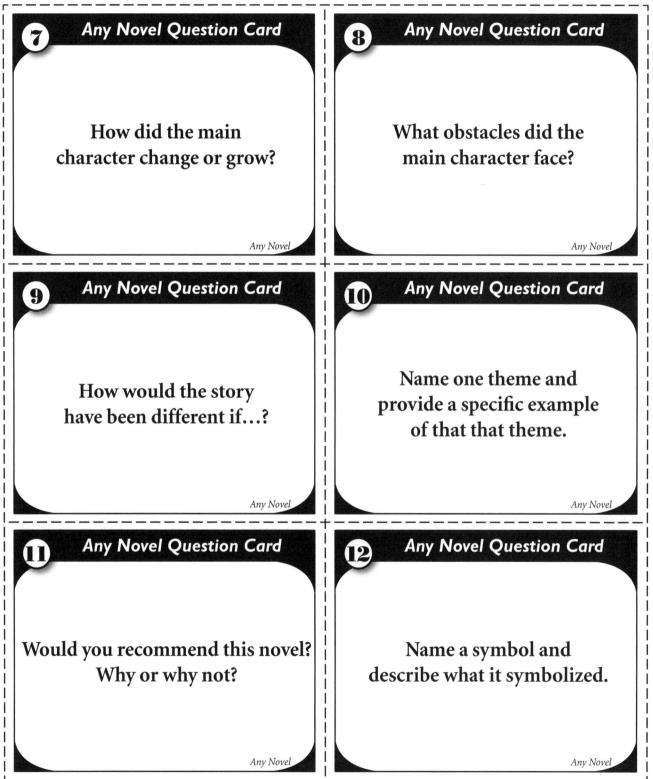

⑦ Any Novel Question Card

How did the main
character change or grow?

Any Novel

⑧ Any Novel Question Card

What obstacles did the
main character face?

Any Novel

⑨ Any Novel Question Card

How would the story
have been different if…?

Any Novel

⑩ Any Novel Question Card

Name one theme and
provide a specific example
of that that theme.

Any Novel

⑪ Any Novel Question Card

Would you recommend this novel?
Why or why not?

Any Novel

⑫ Any Novel Question Card

Name a symbol and
describe what it symbolized.

Any Novel

Poetry Analysis
Question Cards

Directions: Copy enough cards so each student receives a Question Card. Have students stand up, pair up, and do Timed Pair Share to respond to each other's questions. Students trade cards and find a new partner to share.

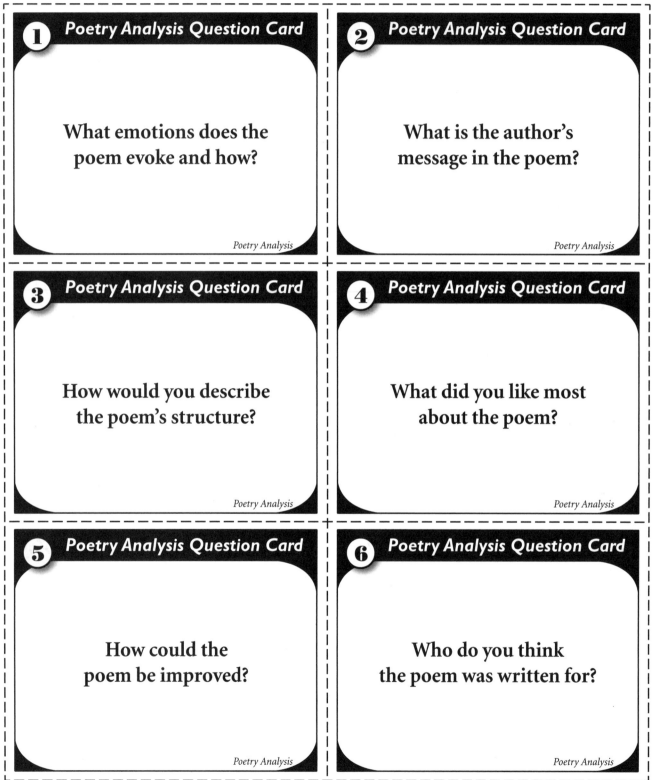

① Poetry Analysis Question Card

What emotions does the
poem evoke and how?

Poetry Analysis

② Poetry Analysis Question Card

What is the author's
message in the poem?

Poetry Analysis

③ Poetry Analysis Question Card

How would you describe
the poem's structure?

Poetry Analysis

④ Poetry Analysis Question Card

What did you like most
about the poem?

Poetry Analysis

⑤ Poetry Analysis Question Card

How could the
poem be improved?

Poetry Analysis

⑥ Poetry Analysis Question Card

Who do you think
the poem was written for?

Poetry Analysis

Poetry Analysis
Question Cards *(continued)*

Directions: Copy enough cards so each student receives a Question Card. Have students stand up, pair up, and do Timed Pair Share to respond to each other's questions. Students trade cards and find a new partner to share.

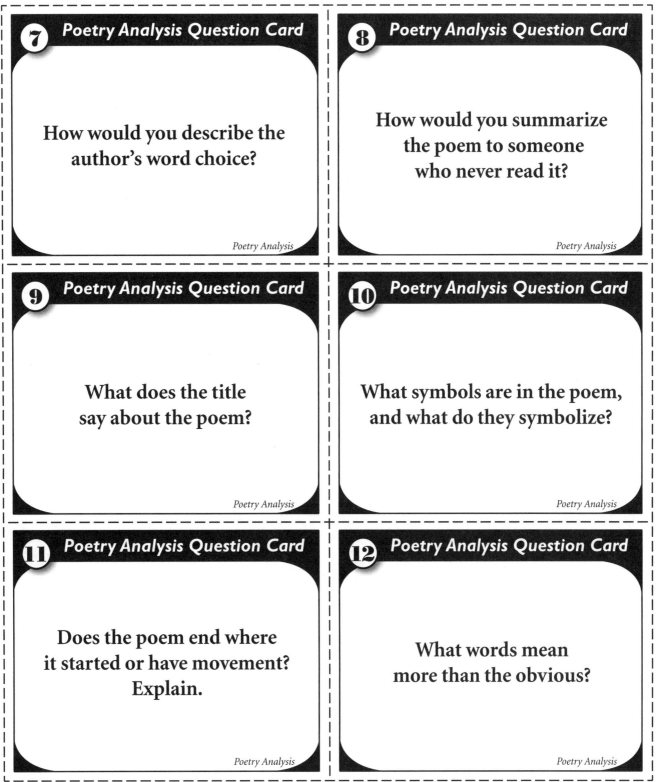

7 Poetry Analysis Question Card

How would you describe the author's word choice?

Poetry Analysis

8 Poetry Analysis Question Card

How would you summarize the poem to someone who never read it?

Poetry Analysis

9 Poetry Analysis Question Card

What does the title say about the poem?

Poetry Analysis

10 Poetry Analysis Question Card

What symbols are in the poem, and what do they symbolize?

Poetry Analysis

11 Poetry Analysis Question Card

Does the poem end where it started or have movement? Explain.

Poetry Analysis

12 Poetry Analysis Question Card

What words mean more than the obvious?

Poetry Analysis

The Giver
Question Cards

Directions: Copy enough cards so each student receives a Question Card. Have students stand up, pair up, and do Timed Pair Share to respond to each other's questions. Students trade cards and find a new partner to share.

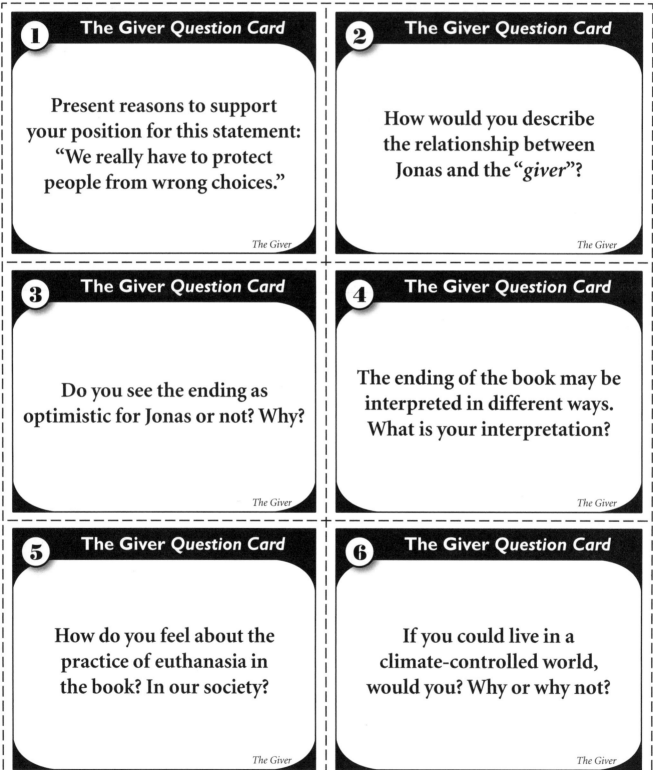

1 The Giver Question Card

Present reasons to support your position for this statement: "We really have to protect people from wrong choices."

The Giver

2 The Giver Question Card

How would you describe the relationship between Jonas and the *"giver"*?

The Giver

3 The Giver Question Card

Do you see the ending as optimistic for Jonas or not? Why?

The Giver

4 The Giver Question Card

The ending of the book may be interpreted in different ways. What is your interpretation?

The Giver

5 The Giver Question Card

How do you feel about the practice of euthanasia in the book? In our society?

The Giver

6 The Giver Question Card

If you could live in a climate-controlled world, would you? Why or why not?

The Giver

The Giver
Question Cards *(continued)*

Directions: Copy enough cards so each student receives a Question Card. Have students stand up, pair up, and do Timed Pair Share to respond to each other's questions. Students trade cards and find a new partner to share.

7 | The Giver Question Card

This community does not appreciate diversity. What value do you see in the diversity within our society?

The Giver

8 | The Giver Question Card

What is your definition of *utopian society*?

The Giver

9 | The Giver Question Card

Is our world becoming more as like or more different from the world in the book?

The Giver

10 | The Giver Question Card

What reasons can you give to support the idea of "release" within the community in *The Giver*?

The Giver

11 | The Giver Question Card

Without true pain, we cannot experience true pleasure. Do you agree or disagree?

The Giver

12 | The Giver Question Card

How does the saying, "ignorance is bliss," apply to this book?

The Giver

Of Mice and Men
Question Cards

Directions: Copy enough cards so each student receives a Question Card. Have students stand up, pair up, and do Timed Pair Share to respond to each other's questions. Students trade cards and find a new partner to share.

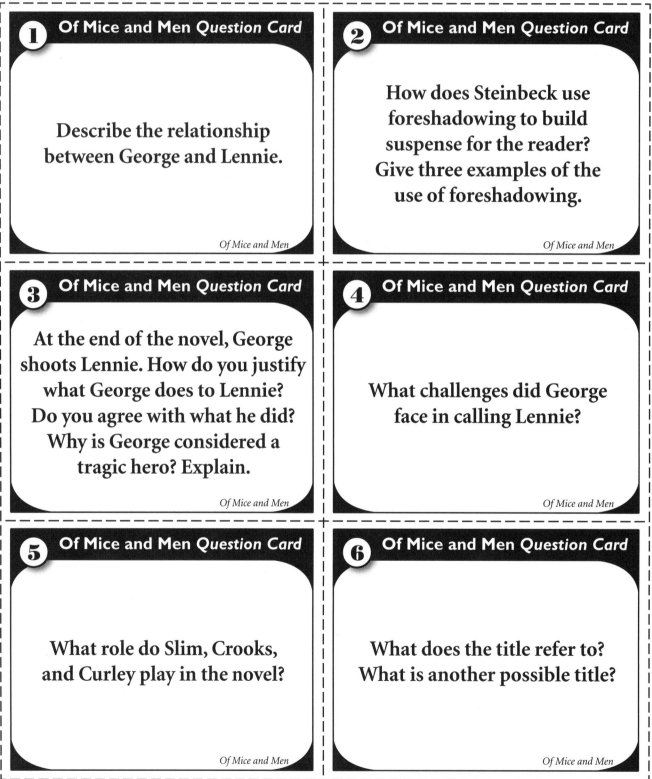

❶ Of Mice and Men *Question Card*

Describe the relationship between George and Lennie.

Of Mice and Men

❷ Of Mice and Men *Question Card*

How does Steinbeck use foreshadowing to build suspense for the reader? Give three examples of the use of foreshadowing.

Of Mice and Men

❸ Of Mice and Men *Question Card*

At the end of the novel, George shoots Lennie. How do you justify what George does to Lennie? Do you agree with what he did? Why is George considered a tragic hero? Explain.

Of Mice and Men

❹ Of Mice and Men *Question Card*

What challenges did George face in calling Lennie?

Of Mice and Men

❺ Of Mice and Men *Question Card*

What role do Slim, Crooks, and Curley play in the novel?

Of Mice and Men

❻ Of Mice and Men *Question Card*

What does the title refer to? What is another possible title?

Of Mice and Men

Of Mice and Men
Question Cards *(continued)*

Directions: Copy enough cards so each student receives a Question Card. Have students stand up, pair up, and do Timed Pair Share to respond to each other's questions. Students trade cards and find a new partner to share.

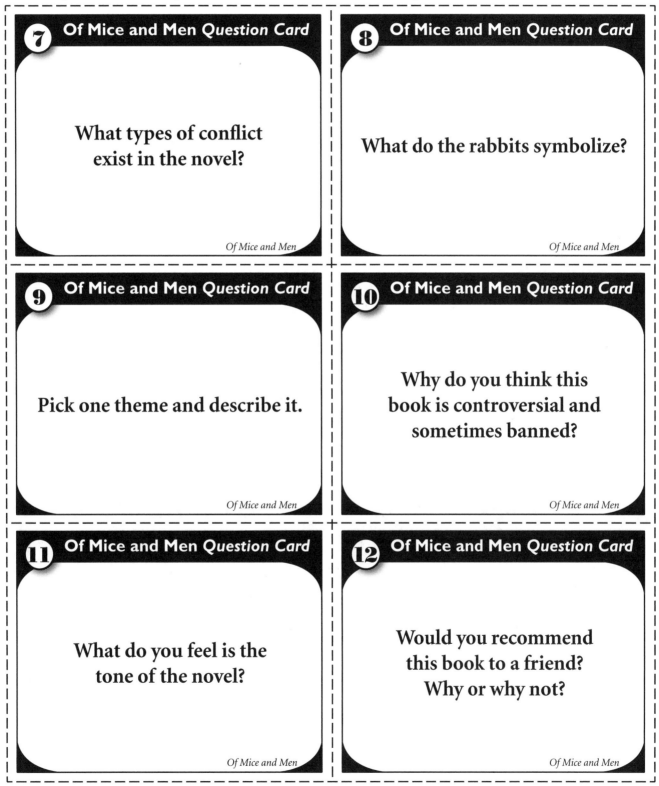

7 *Of Mice and Men Question Card*

What types of conflict exist in the novel?

Of Mice and Men

8 *Of Mice and Men Question Card*

What do the rabbits symbolize?

Of Mice and Men

9 *Of Mice and Men Question Card*

Pick one theme and describe it.

Of Mice and Men

10 *Of Mice and Men Question Card*

Why do you think this book is controversial and sometimes banned?

Of Mice and Men

11 *Of Mice and Men Question Card*

What do you feel is the tone of the novel?

Of Mice and Men

12 *Of Mice and Men Question Card*

Would you recommend this book to a friend? Why or why not?

Of Mice and Men

Blank Question Cards Template

Directions: Copy enough cards for each student. Cut the cards and fold and glue the Question and Answer card back to back. Cards may be laminated for future use.

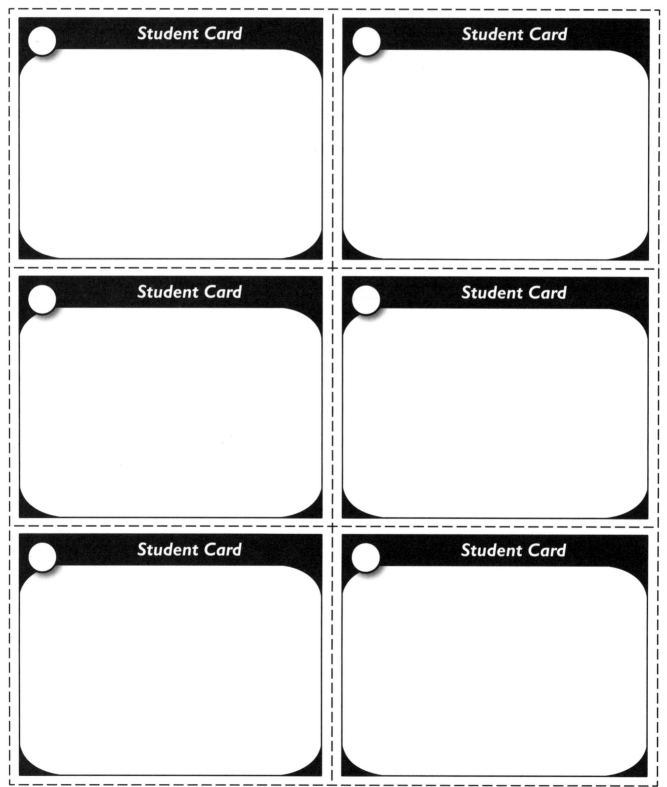

Student Card	Student Card
Student Card	Student Card
Student Card	Student Card